Ebdon's England

Ebdon's England

John Ebdon

DAVID & CHARLES
Newton Abbot   London   North Pomfret (Vt)

British Library Cataloguing in Publication Data

Ebdon, John
  Ebdon's England.
  1. England—Social life and customs—1945–
  I. Title
  942.085'8'0924   DA589.4

  ISBN 0-7153-8595-X

Photoset in Lintron Plantin by
Northern Phototypesetting Co   Bolton
and printed in Great Britain by
A. Wheaton & Co. Ltd, Exeter
for David & Charles (Publishers) Limited
Brunel House   Newton Abbot   Devon

Published in the United States of America
by David & Charles Inc
North Pomfret   Vermont 05053   USA

To Wicked Uncle Chris
(alas beyond recall)
and 'Pook'

Contents

Introduction

To be an Englishman is a singular honour, and in their heart of hearts all sensible foreigners must wish they were one. However, God in His infinite wisdom saw fit to allow only a chosen few of His children to be so privileged. This book is about such people.

God Save The Queen!

1

God Bless the Prince of Wales

'God!' wrote Rupert Brooke of blessed memory, inert church clocks and tea-time honey, 'I must pack and take a train, and get me to England once again. For England', he continued, 'is the one land I know, where men with splendid hearts may go.' He then went on to eulogise about English river smells.

Clearly, and quite properly, Mr Brooke loved and yearned for his country. His intentions and sentiments were unashamedly nationalistic; but they were not original. Messrs C. J. Caesar and A. Plautius entertained and implemented similar thoughts together with a number of close friends, many of whom stayed in our country for several years despite the antipathy toward such tourism displayed by one, Caractacus.

Some went north where, very wisely, they built a substantial wall to distance themselves from the Scots who even then were exhibiting the traits for which they are now famous during the annual encounter between the Glasgow Rangers and Celtic football teams; some paid fleeting visits to the Fen country which they found very flat, and others, with time on their hands, employed themselves by building boringly straight roads, keeping geese, and making the local girls pregnant. Years later they departed with streaming head colds and cursing the English climate; but they were the first to leave their litter on English soil, some of which, in the form of loose change and disposable drinking vessels, is still being uncovered.

Since their departure, and excluding the Scandinavians who arrived smelling strongly of smoked fish and wearing ridiculous hats, there has been a steady flow of visitors to our island. Pakistanis, Indians and West Indians with splendid hearts; Greeks and Cypriots no less well endowed; Arabs and Lebanese. Some of the former have stayed, enriching our culture by bringing the exotic mysteries of the East to the earthiness of Oldham and Huddersfield in the shape of curry powder, yams and breadfruit, while many of the latter have returned to their native countries bearing souvenirs of our civilisation with them, some unknowingly supplied by Harrods, Libertys, Fortnum & Mason and Woolworth's.

Nor should we overlook the invaluable contributions made by our European and transatlantic friends, particularly those from the United States of America. Not only have they helped to bolster our troubled economy, they have enlivened our vocabulary with new words. To them we are indebted for 'weatherwise', 'healthwise', 'moneywise' and 'workwise'. We have become flush with sapience. Conversely, if our cash flow fails to correspond with our thru'put we may find ourselves privatised, hospitalised, or at best, in need of medication. In short, our dialogue has become much more meaningful.

Not all Englishmen have approved of these importations from across the Atlantic. Indeed, a faction of our countrymen have even been heard to say that in their opinion the discovery of America was a grave error of judgement and are quick to point out that it was a Portuguese who committed the blunder; but theirs is a minority voice.

Such resistance to new speech patterns is understandable. By tradition we are a conservative people, proud of our heritage and geographical isolation from the rest of the world. We do not take readily to change of any kind. In retrospect, therefore, much credit is due to the catering staff of the House of Commons, who, in 1973, struck a daring blow for European unity. Members of Parliament returning after the Christmas recess were greeted with a continental touch to mark Britain's entry into the Common Market. A new à la carte menu was presented to them. It contained, among other dishes, frogs' legs at 50p per portion, and snails in the shell at 70p the half dozen. Both delicacies, they were advised, would be served in a garlic sauce.

The innovation received a mixed reception. Pro-marketeers and monarchists applauded the gesture. Garlic, they said, was well known to be a powerful aphrodisiac. Historians, they enlightened their political opponents privily, had recorded that Henry IV, a monarch famous for his virility, daily had cracked a clove of it between his teeth. 'Possibly,' rejoined the opposition, 'but were not the Honourable Members aware that the same chroniclers had also disclosed that His Majesty's breath could fell an ox at twenty paces? Furthermore', they continued, 'were not the Honourable Members cognisant of the fact that the mere *smell* of the bulb had been known to cause persons to over-salivate? That it had an effect on them not dissimilar to that experienced by trumpet players when confronted by

11

lemon suckers? Were they ignorant', they pressed, 'of the sad case of the opera singer, Maria Callas, who, when embraced by a jealous and wantonly garlic-chewing tenor during a love duet could only dribble the aria and, moreover, lost her curtain call? And lastly, would not the Honourable Gentlemen concede that if this foreign addition to the menu continued, the House could be faced with the prospect of a rampant front bench, a slavering opposition, and a total collapse of the British parliamentary system? Surely then', they concluded, 'in the interests of democracy, it should be withdrawn if not outlawed throughout the country.' English fare, they advanced, was good enough for them.

These exchanges were conducted in the lobbies of Westminster. Debate never reached the floor of the House. Consequently no mention of the issue appeared in *Hansard*, but the topic did not enjoy an easy death. There will always be a nucleus of die-hards opposed to the encroachment of anything foreign into the English way of life, and this was no exception. However, eventually, albeit grudgingly, even they accepted the logic of those who endorsed Mark Twain's maxim that part of the secret of success in this life is to eat what you like and let the food fight it out inside, and that in the interests of tourism it was essential to establish a rapport with our overseas visitors and to pander to their eating habits. England, it was pointed out to them, had much to attract the foreign tourist, but English culinary skill was not one of the inducements. Brown Windsor soup, it was argued, did little to excite a Parisian's taste buds despite the oblique suggestion that it had a royal blessing; even Germans found it boring.

God Bless the Prince of Wales

The decision was a wise one and its implementation has had a marked effect on the growth of the tourist industry. No longer is the potential visitor to our shores put off by the thought of having to endure a diet of watery greens, over-cooked potatoes and toad in or out of the hole. Now every national may come to the capital assured that, gastronomically at least, his whims will be satisfied. London has become a gourmet's paradise and no palate need leave it unrequited. Moreover, as any Saudi returning from a shop-lifting spree in Oxford Street will see, the subject of food and diet control is now of paramount interest to the English. They will happen upon a Mr Stanley Charlie Green.

Mr Green is a gaunt, melancholy, bespectacled man with a dirty raincoat, whose mission in life is to dissuade his fellows, particularly women, from eating protein.

'Are you', he inquires mournfully of passing housewives, 'too passionate for your husband? Are you', he asks of his startled audience, 'bad-tempered, and made to say harsh words to them? If so', he counsels in tones from the tomb, 'try less protein. That will moderate your Pashy-on. Your husband will think he's got a new wife. And', he continues, as their colour heightens and they quicken their step, 'you'll be so nice – again.'

Mr Green, presumably mindful of the axiom that a moving target is harder to hit than a stationary one, keeps on the move as he intones his litany. 'Meat . . . fish . . . birds and cheese . . . beans, peas, eggs and lentils – all spell Pashy-on, and are bad. Especially len-tools,' he drones, unwilling to relinquish his hold on the last syllable, 'there's lechery in len-tools . . .'

Only once did I see him get a bad press. An irate young

woman, undoubtedly satiated with fish and peas, called him a vegetarian ponce and banged on his sandwich board. He eyed her dispassionately. 'See what I mean?' he inquired of us lugubriously. 'It's the meat in her, that's what it is – the meat.'

England should be proud of Stanley Charlie Green. His converts, if any, are few, and in no way has he embarrassed the markets of Covent Garden and Smithfield by his proselytising; nor has there been a marked drop in the sale of lentils. But in Oxford Street, together with another encased gentleman who over the years has served notice that the end of the world is nigh and who, by the law of averages will one day be correct, Mr Green has won the hearts of tourists in general, and of the Americans in particular. 'Jees!' they say when he first appears in their field of vision, 'grab this cookie, Patsy – this we must have!' And before he knows where he is, Stanley Charlie Green has been immortalised on celluloid and exported to Illinois together with a London policeman and a Beefeater. He is one of London's greatest contributions to tourism, as popular as Madame Tussaud's and second only to the Royal Family.

Unlike Mr William Hamilton, once described as one of Scotland's less attractive sons, Americans are very fond of our Royal Family. They hunger for news about them, digesting every proffered morsel no matter how small, how dated or, in the case of information gleaned from continental magazines, how inaccurate. And we, to our credit, now do our best to feed their appetites.

It has been said that two World Wars immeasurably improved the Englishman's knowledge of geography. It is equally true that the annual invasion of North Americans has occasioned and markedly increased our scholarship of our own history and lineage of the Royal Family. Facts, which prior to the arrival of package tours from the New World would have passed unknown and unremarked upon, have been unearthed, retained and used to satisfy their curiosity. Moreover, the good people from Tennessee and Texas have helped indirectly to lessen one problem of unemployment. Many a Master or Bachelor of Arts with an ability to absorb and deliver historical trivia through a hand microphone has been plucked from our lengthening dole queues and employed as a tourist guide. They too do a fine job for England and may be seen and heard exampling their expertise in the very heart of the capital.

'The statue at which you are looking', said such a person within my earshot and addressing an admiring group before the west door of St Paul's Cathedral, 'is of Queen Anne.' 'Yeah,' said a voice from the Bronx, 'she's dead.' His informant gave him a wintery smile. 'Quite so,' he said; and cleared his throat. 'They say unkindly of that statue', he resumed, 'that she stands with her back to the church and her face' – and here he gestured to a nearby hostelry – 'in that pub over there. You see', he continued, regardless of washing dirty royal linen in public, 'Queen Anne tippled.'

'No kiddin',' said the man from the Bronx, 'ya mean she was a wino?' His. mentor looked upon him with disfavour. 'Brandy,' he said shortly. 'Queen Anne was very fond of brandy.' 'Yeah?' said the man from the Bronx producing a hip flask, 'with me it's Bourbon.' 'We know,' said his wife, a hennaed lady wearing non-reflecting sunglasses, 'now lay off and listen to the guy,

15

stoopid. Go on, mister,' she said encouragingly, 'so she drank, huh?' 'She did, madame', reiterated the historian extraordinaire, 'but', he added, 'she had every excuse. She had seventeen children.'

A gasp went up from the women in the assembly. 'Seven*teen*,' said one, incredulously, her jaws momentarily stilled in their attack upon a wad of gum, 'what, all by the same guy?' '*All*', confirmed her expositor firmly, diplomatically adapting her idiom, 'by the same, er, guy. Prince George', he said, nominating the Royal gentleman at stud, 'her Consort.' 'Jees!' said the man from the Bronx, refreshing himself from his flask, 'good for Annie. Some broad, huh? I guess –' 'But none of her children', interrupted their dragoman, ignoring the slight upon the deceased monarch, 'survived her. After all those attempts', he continued sombrely, 'she died without an heir. It was', he concluded sorrowfully, 'a great disappointment to them.'

'Maybe, buster,' said the man from the Bronx, 'but they sure had fun trying! Say – when did the guy eat?'

When I parted from them, the cicerone was still holding his own, but with difficulty. The gentleman from the Bronx belligerently and insistently was offering him his flask, and two blue-rinsed ladies in purple slacks, motivated by the thought of Queen Anne's seventeen confinements and subsequent fall from grace, were arguing with him over the ethics and efficacy of legalised abortion and the use of the pill. But despite these trials he was still smiling bravely and upholding the flag.

Like that of Gilbert's policeman, the lot of a London tourist guide is not always a happy one. Many show signs of strain by the end of a season; but all stick manfully to their guns knowing that they are playing a vital role in shaping the future of our country. Tourism is now big business. It is an industry and is being recognised as such; even by Punks in the King's Road, Chelsea. They too have come to terms with reality, as did the Masai, that much-photographed minority tribe in East Africa who, complete with cow dung and ochre in their hair, were wont to pose gratis before the world's cameras, but no longer do so. Sticky with hair lacquer, imported dyes and stale perspiration, our Punks emulate those splendid tribesmen and refuse to face French lenses free of charge for a snapshot of 'Le Mohican'. 'No! No!' they cry, shaking their thrice-pierced ornamented ears. 'One-fifty, or else get knotted!' 'Ah,' say the French, 'ah, les Smarts! Les Anglais Punks! Ils sont très drôles, n'est-ce-pas?' And they pay up without a murmur.

Nor is the average man in the street unmindful of his duty. No longer does he shy at the sight of a caftan or a burnous, or flinch at the sound of a foreign tongue asking to be directed to 'Bookenhum Palis' or 'Li-ces-taire Squaire'. Admittedly he will continue to assume, as his forebears did, that all foreigners are deaf or mentally defective and will shout at them, but he no longer cuts them dead. Now, the discerning patriot will acknowledge and rejoice in the foreigners' existence, knowing that with their tangible presence comes England's economic salvation – the invisible export. England, he will muse, may be ASLEF'd, NUR'd, and even NUM'd, but while the foreigners come with their dollars and deutschmarks, there is hope for Britannia yet. And C of E or Methodist, Catholic or fashionable agnostic, all will pray for the continuance of the Royal line: for Royal wedding feasts and births, and Troopings of the Colour; events which no other country can match, the peerless pageantry of English pomp and ceremony which sets the tills a-ringing. And their minds will go back to 1981 to the year of the Royal Wedding, and the halcyon days of tourism.

No Englishman will easily forget the euphoria which greeted the news that Prince Charles was to marry Lady Diana Spencer. Grey February was brightened and lord and commoner alike applauded the announcement; but none more enthusiastically than those in the tourist trade. And rightly so, for it was a happening destined to fill our hearts with pride, and our hotels with visitors. Boom time came to Britain.

The wheels of industry, oiled and galvanised into life by the coming nuptials, filled shop windows to capacity with objets d'art and trash. Noses were blown on Lady Di, plates were dried on Lady Di, coats and keys were hung on the Prince, cigarettes stubbed on Royal faces and trousers suspended from Royal braces. And in downtown souvenir land one could even wear a Royal Couple bra.

Wedding fever gripped the capital, and its population swelled as thousands flooded into it, drawn by the monarchical magnet. Outside Madame Tussaud's, within whose halls a waxen Lady Di stared glassily toward her Royal in-laws elect, the leeches of London methodically milked the queues. Bereft of teeth and with his hat in his hand, the resident mouth-organ player chauvinistically dribbled a tuneless travesty of the National Anthem and gummily asked God to bless his tone-deaf donors; the Jumping Bean man rolled his wares around his tray – patriotic Jumping Beans in red and white and blue and freshly marked up by 50 per cent in honour of the occasion; and on the corner by the adjoining Planetarium, the Monkey Man made a killing. Draped with long-tailed, smelly and pathetic apes, he gave his victims little chance. As quick as a flash he would have one on them, just as swiftly arrange a pose, and away they went with a drying print and £1.50 the poorer. 'God bless the Prince of Wales!' he would cry, 'God Bless the Prince and Lady Di!' and disappear into a pub. He had, to quote one of England's former leading statesmen, 'never had it so good'; and I said as much to a donnish clergyman friend of mine who had watched the overall activities with me.

'Yes,' he said thoughtfully, with an eye on the still growing queues, 'His Highness and Di are doing us proud. But you know, my dear John, a macabre thought has just occurred to me. Suppose', said he, 'that in tomorrow's Court Page of *The Times* we read "the marriage arranged between you-know-her and you-know-who, will not now take place . . ." ' and he opened his eyes wide behind his spectacles. 'Let us pray,' he said.

My friend, by virtue of his cloth, must remain anonymous. Suffice it to say that he is one of the oldest minor Clerks in Holy Orders in the Anglican Communion and unlikely to be relieved of the status in the foreseeable future.

Promotion has always escaped him, and will continue to do so. Despite having a keen academic brain (1st Class Hons, Balliol) a small private income and unimpeachably sound theology – never once has he questioned the authenticity of the Virgin Birth or the authority of the Conservative Party to govern by Divine Right – bishops have never smiled upon him. Unfortunately for his ecclesiastical career, and despite these invaluable credits, he has one trait which has alienated him from the hierarchy of the Church of England. He is possessed of a bizarre sense of humour. It is not, for example, every visiting Archdeacon who takes kindly to being served with a plastic fried egg for his breakfast, let alone being forced to side-step what in joke shops are marketed under the label 'Dirty Fido' or 'Bad Dog Rover'. 'That', they mutter as they take their leave of him, 'is not our sort of fun.' And they voice their views abroad.

I am very fond of my friend. We share many interests, astronomy being one of our joint pursuits; but I confess to being easily led by him. Under his influence and in the words of the *Book of Common Prayer*, I have done those things which I ought not to have done. I will not enumerate all my indiscretions; it would not be politic to do so, or seemly. But it was through my friend that I became a waxwork.

'Come!' I cried that fateful day, knowing that he had never been to Madame Tussaud's, 'let's go and look at the Royal Bride.' And exercising my right as Director of the adjoining Planetarium, I took him in by the back stairs.

He was much impressed. Together, and in the company of a throng of other visitors, we gazed at the famous and the infamous who uncomplainingly stared back. We heard 'oohs!' and 'aahs!' around Lady Di, and the clicks of the Nikons and Pentax and Zeiss. We watched a Greek Cypriot cross himself before Makarios; saw a cloth-capped gentleman put his tongue out at Mrs Thatcher, and observed a rangy Australian being mesmerised by Barbara Cartland's bosoms.

'My oath,' he twanged, unable to take his eyes from the chiffon-pink, rhinestone-shimmering mass before him,

'Get those charlies, Dawn! Strewth! You wouldn't get many of those in a kilo.' 'Don't be so bloody crude, Jacko,' snapped his companion, digging him in the T-shirt with her elbow, 'doncha know she's Lady Di's stepgran?'

Understandably, the experience left its mark on my friend. He spoke about it at length during supper that evening. He thought many of the figures were very good. Indeed he pronounced some to be excellent. But it was their therapeutic value which had impressed him most.

'Where else', said he rhetorically, and harking back to the Thatcher baiter and the boob-bemused Antipodean, 'can one face ones *bêtes noires* and give them the two fingers? And *know*', he pursued, 'that they can't retaliate?' 'I agree,' I said, 'it's a great innovation. Relieves the blood pressure no end.' 'Um,' he said, 'should be on the National Health, old boy.' He sipped thoughtfully at his Margaux. 'But suppose,' he postulated, replacing his glass, 'just suppose that they *could* talk back? I mean, suppose for instance, that old Maggie suddenly uttered? You know, just like that?' And he raised his eyebrows toward his hairline. 'Gosh,' he said, 'that'd clear the room, my Lord it would!' He took up his wine once more and giggled into it. 'Oh my Lord,' he repeated joyously, 'that *would* be fun!' And he sipped again and eyed me quizzically across the rim. 'Huh! huh!' he said. 'Huh! huh!'

I have known my friend for many years. Uneasily and intuitively I knew what was coming; and saw horns sprout from his head.

'I don't suppose', he asked softly, 'that *you've* ever thought of being a waxwork? Have you? Just for a few

21

minutes?'

As I have said, I am easily led.

My life as a waxwork was a short but immensely interesting one and a role which I would recommend to any student of human nature. Admittedly, I enjoyed certain advantages. Structurally the London Planetarium is connected to the exhibition by a labyrinth of corridors and I knew the venue well. Secondly, the uniformed attendants knew me and outwardly evinced no surprise when I appraised them of my plan. 'Of course Sir,' they said, exchanging pitying looks, 'of course you want to be a waxwork – don't we all?' And courteous fellows that they were, they co-operated splendidly.

The great room which houses the massed figures of the mighty is only a part of the Tussaud's complex. There are alcoves and annexes, and *en route* for the Grand Hall one happens upon many a solitary waxen notable in unexpected places. Some lean over ballustrades, others sit engrossed in reading newspapers, and one or two informally engage in conversation; but all appear relaxed. It was within this area that I positioned myself.

Unless one is a graduate of the school of Transcendental Meditation and capable of studying one's navel for hours or accustomed to long periods of advanced yoga, it is not easy to be a waxwork. Clearly one has to exercise an iron control over all parts of one's body. One must not move. It is, therefore, of paramount importance to ensure beforehand that one will not be incommoded in any way during one's vigil and, once *in situ*, to adopt as comfortable a pose as possible. After much deliberation and rehearsal before the mirror in the gentlemen's lavatory, I elected to stand with my feet astride, my hands upon my hips, and to gaze into the distance with a *sans peur et sans reprôche* expression. And there I stood; and waited.

I was not kept long in suspense. A small boy with impetigo stood before me, and drank in what he saw. 'Mum,' he inquired, ''ose this?' 'I dunno,' said Mum through a mouthful of crisps, 'some geezer. Why?' 'Because', said the child, ''e's gotta nair coming out of his nose.' 'Coo, yes,' said Mum closing in for a better look, 'so 'e 'as. Real in'it? Marvellous what they can do.'

It was a promising start, but there was better to come. After a brief lull which enabled me to draw breath and blink my eyes, and as the perspiration soaked slowly into my collar, I was poked thrice, tweaked twice and orally assaulted once. But it was the last indignity which I remember most vividly.

For reasons best known to himself, a large German gentleman with a generous mouth and wearing rimless glasses and a hostile expression stopped before me, and stared. Then, running his fingers quickly across his lips from north to south, went 'Boodley-boodley-boodley-boodley-boo!'

What the gesture did for him I shall never know; but I recall what it did for me. It broke my concentration. I stopped being a waxwork. Moreover, not only did I move; I uttered. Forcibly.

'Pooh!' I said, and put out my tongue.

I still relish that moment. The Teutonic one all but left his shoes, an Italian lady called loudly upon God to come to her aid, two French girls clung to each other, and an English voice said it was 'disgusting' and that 'they' should be ashamed of themselves. And I, I must own, had hysterics.

23

I still relish that moment

However, all ended happily. Stickily we all shook hands and diplomatic relations were restored. The Italian lady stopped fanning herself and les demoiselles recovered, the Berliner went out of my life, smiling and promising that his grandchildren should know of the day when he had been 'zurprized by ze vax', and I returned to my office, pleased that I had accepted the challenge. Not only had it been an unusual experience, the experiment had confirmed a theory of mine that regardless of their age or nationality, all tourists, including the British, must touch things, and particularly objects displayed beneath large signs reading DO NOT TOUCH. It is an irrepressible urge, as forceful as Ben Gunn's craving for cheese, and there is no stopping it.

The compulsion is international. Moreover, it is a trait which appears to go hand in hand with another much exercised by tourists, namely that written instructions of any kind – even those posted in their mother tongue – do not apply to them, and should be ignored.

I have seen this exampled many times and was afforded further evidence of the endemicity on my way back to the Planetarium. I passed a group of people all smoking happily under a multi-language sign advising them that smoking was forbidden; I watched an irate man banging angrily upon a glass door inscribed 'please use the other door'; and later, under the Planetarium dome as I prepared to introduce the uninitiated to the silent celestial beauties of the heavens, I listened to the noisy terrestrial rhythmic licking of illegal cornets and heard the crackling of forbidden crisps. Mercifully the sounds of mass salivation and crunching died shortly after the setting of an artificial sun, but at its onset I looked toward the coming of the night with some temerity and wondered how I would reach the dawn.

The London Planetarium is as much an English institution as Madame Tussaud's or the Tower of London, and I hold it in great affection. I joined its staff in 1960 as a narrator and eventually, and in a manner not dissimilar to the way in which I achieved seniority in the Royal Air Force, ie by outliving my friends and outwitting my enemies, I became its Director.

My appointment would have delighted the nanny of my early childhood for it was she who introduced me to astronomy. She was a lovable person possessed of three consuming interests: gin; the stars; and myself; and in that order of priority. Consequently, nearly every star she saw was a binary, and most of the planets and constellations which swam into her ken were blurred at the edges; but it was through her that my appetite for the subject was whetted.

'I could not sleep for thinking of the sky' wrote Masefield in his Lollington Downs, 'the unending sky with all its million suns . . .' So it has been with me. Since childhood I have looked at and thought about the sky. It is a profitable exercise and one which I once commended to a man in the Planetarium.

'Sod that for a lark,' he said unpleasantly, 'I haven't paid to be made to think'; and he rose from his seat in high dudgeon. Plainly he found the suggestion abhorrent and I suspect that had he embraced the idea it would have proved a unique experience for him. But he, poor man, whose reddened eyes I hazard had never looked higher than a television screen, had missed much in life. The heavens are rich in food for thought.

God Bless the Prince of Wales

One can think of how, when and by whom the constellations were first named; of the myths and legends surrounding them. One can think of the fact that every bright star has a name of its own: Alcyone, Merope, Maia, Electra; Aldebaran, Deneb and Saiph; some from the Arabic, some from the Greek; that above one's head in the world of stars there is the teen-aged, middle-aged, babe and ancient; hot stars, cold stars, giants and dwarfs; great globes of gas speeding through space, some coming toward us, others moving away, and every one a sun. But perhaps the most humbling thought is this:

We look out from one planet which, with eight others, is moving around one star; our sun. One star of a hundred thousand million others which make up the cartwheeling, spiral galaxy in which, by chance or design, we live. And that galaxy itself, the edge of which we see as a faint river of light running across the heavens and call the Milky Way, is but one of a thousand million other stellar cities in the universe of stars. And Man? A mere speck upon a dot in the cosmos. But specks though we be, we are blessed with intelligence; and many other gifts. Among them is the precious one of sight. Most of us take it for granted. I did, until temporarily I was relieved of it during the war. It was a salutory lesson. And when I regained my sight, I looked upon the things of the Earth, and of the heavens, with a fresh awareness.

The night sky has always had a hold upon me. I have looked upon it from the Cyclades and with the passing of the hours watched the Grecian heroes rise and set, their figures outlined in the constellations; I have seen the flaming kite of the Southern Cross dragging its tail from a southern sea; and lying on my back in the Kenyan bush I have stretched out my hand and in imagination plucked the Hyades from their setting and touched the Seven Sisters as the cicadas sang in the still clear night.

What skies they were! And would that we in England were so blessed with their constant clarity. But our skies mourn for much of the year and drape themselves with cloud, and on the clear nights that we are allowed, street lighting and industrial haze robs town dwellers of their beauty. Hence, the value of the Planetarium. There, under its vast copper dome, weathered green by England's dreadful elements, one can sit back and watch an imitation heaven fill with stars yet still be unaware of its artificiality. And for many, the experience is their first brush with astronomy.

However, not all visit the establishment intent upon astronomical enlightenment. Some, apprised by word of mouth that within its circle they may sit down, go in because their feet are killing them; some, lacking terrestrial orientation enter it mistakenly and leave perplexed that they saw no waxen figures; and a small number of carnal couples patronise it knowing that darkness will be their shield. I have heard, and in the half-light witnessed, dreadful things being done under the stars of Virgo or when the moon was full, activities which proved to me the remarkable insight of the minor poet who wrote:

Under the star-decked vault of heaven
We love-drenched mortals do the strangest things.

There are also those misinformed occasionals who take their seats and patiently await the splitting of the dome in

28

twain. This, they have been advised mistakenly, is the means by which they will be shown the splendours of the heavens as seen from above the lowering clouds under which they entered the building. One such was an Oriental gentleman who, in the spring of 1969, and despite the assurances of an elderly attendant that he would not be soaked *en route* for Elysium, remained seated under an open umbrella. Reluctantly, and still disbelieving, he lowered it shortly before the Summer Solstice. However, he left the auditorium marvelling not only at his dry condition but at what he had witnessed. His eyes had been opened. So too, are those of the majority who visit the Planetarium. True, they may make their exits with stiffened neck muscles and the feeling that they have spent a lifetime in the dentist's chair, but they take with them a painless appreciation of the vastness of space and of their place within it. Nevertheless, not all leave happily. Prudent though I am with my choice of words when evangelising to the public, and forever mindful of the higher illiteracy with which many of our young are afflicted, regretfully and unwittingly, I sometimes give offence.

'And there, ladies and gentlemen,' I said impressively one bright May morning as I pointed to a tiny moving dot of light in motion around a stationary sun, 'there goes the Earth, our place in space – the home of homo sapiens. Homo sapiens,' I repeated, 'Man the Wise.'

Below me in the dark came the noise of a child whispering to its mother, quickly followed by the sound of its head being smacked. Rustling with outrage its dam glared at me through the gloom. 'I don't care what that man in the box said,' she shrilled, 'if *you* ever use that word again you'll go straight to bed.' And so saying, she dragged her grizzling offspring unceremoniously across the laps and feet of a couple of nuns and away from further oral pollution. 'Holy Mother!' said one of the Sisters to the background clatter of scattering beads, 'He's done for me rosary, that's for sure! Oh dear! oh dear! oh dear!'

Voluminous in her habit, she rose from her seat like a great black bat and peered at me across the console top. 'Professor,' said she in a sibilant whisper as more beads left her person and rained to the floor, 'd'you think you could put up the lights?' 'Reverend Mother,' said I in an undertone, 'do you think you could wait just a while? It's only ten minutes to sunrise.' 'Sure, sure', she hissed as the cascade ceased, and sank silently out of sight.

Two nebulae and four galaxies later we began the search for her beads to which Protestants and Catholics alike from the surrounding seats lent their assistance. It was a remarkable display of Christian togetherness and church unity. Miraculously all fifty-five were recovered. So too was a plastic button, five smarties in assorted colours, and an imitation jade earring. Excluding the button, all were claimed and their Reverences left giving thanks to everyone, and to St Anthony in particular. But they returned. Moreover, on their second pilgrimage they brought with them 240 girls from the Convent School at which they taught. Fortunately for my staff and the smooth running of the presentation, none were wearing rosaries.

Much of the Planetarium's annual intake of visitors is made up of school parties. Not all are shepherded by nuns, but those that are are remarkable for their politeness and attentiveness; and with good reason. The slightest act of indiscipline is dealt with summarily, and many a crack and smack have I heard reverberating in the dark as a well placed crucifix, swung on its chain, found an irreverent set of knuckles. The Sisters of Mercy show little tolerance for any ill manners displayed by their flocks. Unfortunately, the same cannot be said for some of the teaching staff doing penance in our East End secondary and comprehensive schools. Often considerably smaller in stature than their charges, these tutorial unfortunates are readily recognisable. Many twitch and glance uneasily over their shoulders, and all have aged prematurely. My heart bleeds for them. But even their pupils fall under the spell of space and they soon stop slashing the seats.

Many and varied are the children of England who come to look at the stars. Some are keen and bright and eager; some are nice, and some are horrid; but all present a challenge. And none more so than the Gifted Child.

England is fortunate to have her Gifted Children. Blessed with an intelligence quotient well beyond their years and an insatiable curiosity compared with which Kipling's Elephant's Child would appear world weary, those reaching adulthood, and not forced by a stunted English technology to leave for more enterprising foreign fields, will do their country proud. But they are a demanding, questing section of England's youth, and not easily satisfied intellectually. I know. Regularly, once a year in early January, 400 of these prodigiosities, together with their less gifted parents, assemble and await me in the Planetarium. And I, recovering from the excesses of the Christmas festivities, await them.

My preparations for the occasion never vary. On the night before Philippi, I take to my bed early, and on the morning of the engagement allow myself the luxury of two minutes of silent prayer prior to confronting the restless sea of brilliance before me. Thus, fortified physically and spiritually, I enter the console, take a deep breath, wait for silence; and throw the book at their Gifted Heads.

I pronounce on the theories of Newton, and Einstein, propound about pulsars and quasars and quarks; I hold forth about black holes, gamma and X-rays, enthuse over nebulae, novae and neutrons; I fill their gifted lives with galaxies, gas, and galactic clusters, drench them in light-years and take them to the planets, and then finally, as my adrenal glands cry 'halt!', I await their gifted questions. I am never kept long in suspense. Nor have I ever ceased to be struck by the depth and catholicity of the interrogation.

Do I, as an astronomer, believe in God, and if so why? Is Patrick Moore like that all the time? Do I not think that as we evolve into technological giants there is a danger of us becoming spiritual dwarfs? Why do I use a light-year when a parsec is so much simpler? What do I think about astrology? And lastly, and most frequently, and invariably delivered in urgent tones 'Where's the toilet?'

I am very fond of the Gifted Child. No country should be without one. Or even two. Furthermore, their annual visit is one to which I look forward, eagerly. But as a Beta in this Brave New World and conscious of my own intellectual limitations and advancing years, I am glad that the event is not a monthly fixture. I am not a selfish person, but one of my dearest wishes is to live long enough to be cared for, and cherished by, my own much loved but very ordinary children.

The English child, cerebral or gnostically unre-markable, is welcomed at the Planetarium, and their numbers are legion. But between the months of June and September, it is the foreign visitor who is in the majority there, and throughout the capital. It is the time when the litter deepens in our streets and when many a guardsman at Buckingham Palace is poked and provoked by alien Alices. But never let us cease to give thanks for the presence of this force from overseas; and for their wallets and purses. For with this continuance of foreign aid an edentate British lion may get new dentures and roar once more instead of lisping at the world. And who knows? Perhaps one day in the House of Commons, some future Chancellor of the Exchequer, flushed with triumph and watered whisky, will snap shut his battered budget box and cry 'God for Charlie! England, and St George!', and knock 10p off the standard rate of Income Tax.

But this is the stuff of which dreams are made. In reality, and in essence, the Budget Speech, that hardiest of English fiscal flora which often blooms twice yearly, will remain as constant through the coming years as it has through past decades. This is no idle speculation. The context of the Budget Speech is traditional; *Hansard* and political historians have recorded this steadfastness; so too has the wireless set.

Thanks to the courtesy of the British Broadcasting Corporation (whom God Preserve) I was afforded the opportunity of listening to every recorded budget broadcast made and preserved in wax between 1931 and 1968. I heard the voices of past Prime Ministers and Chancellors, all rich in platitude, and sepia with melancholy, crackle at me from the discs. All told me a similar story. It was a sombre experience and taxing on the ear, but the aural exercise led me to conclude that no government spokesperson of the future need expend time and energy in preparing a fresh broadcast budgetary statement to the nation. In co-operation with the BBC, a unikit address could be compiled, recorded and played over the air; a montage of bursal voices from the past, an authoritative vocal assembly.

Admittedly, the preparation of such a presentation would be no easy task. Much care would need to be exercised in the choice of speakers, and in the winnowing of the gathered material. Not all could be used, but the discerning selector would soon become aware of an emerging pattern. He would note that all speakers – regardless of the political colours of their governments – were careful to stress, and explain, the following facts:

1. That although the economic situation was parlous, it was *not* the fault of the government.
2. The reasons *why* the nation's finances were in disarray.
3. The urgency with which they should be prevented from becoming worse.
4. How the miracle could be achieved, and lastly, that every man, woman and child should remember that the worst could not possibly happen, because they were British.

With strict adherence to these mandatory and well-tested guidelines and an occasional reference to God, I am confident that the manufacture of such a broadcast would be of inestimable benefit to the nation. But I am a realist. I accept that it may take many years before this revolutionary concept is embraced; that I shall not live to see it come to fruition. Nevertheless, with deference, and as a good Englishman with my country's interests at heart, I have devised a format which will, I hope, be given earnest and sympathetic governmental consideration. Involving the usage of the texts and voices of no more than ten of the cream of Britain's bygone budgeting orators, but not necessarily in chronological order, the peroration would be finished in under six minutes, and begin thus:

Announcer 'This is London. Today is Budget Day. Here is the Chancellor of the Exchequer to explain his Budget.' *Pause.*

Sir John Simon (1939) 'This is Budget Day. And on Budget Day the House of Commons begins its survey of our National Accounts and considers how the expenses which Great Britain incurs during the year can be met. I am glad to have the opportunity of making as plain as I can the essential facts and figures.' *Pause.*

Mr Clement Attlee (1947) 'I have no easy words for you tonight. You all know the serious economic position of our country; but I want to hold your interest, and to stir your imagination. I have a heavy responsibility upon me, but you have too.' *Pause.*

Sir Stafford Cripps (1949) 'Do you remember last year I told you we had to take special measures to stop the dangers of inflation? It's been with us more or less ever since before the first World War; but it's become much more intense since the last war, and indeed in the last few months, has become very, *very* serious indeed.'

Mr Neville Chamberlain (1936) 'I cannot flatter myself that the story I have to tell you about this year's budget will be as agreeable to you as the one I told you a year ago.

35

But that is not *my* fault.'

Mr Ramsay Macdonald (1931) 'The world depression in trade has hit all countries very hard. Including ourselves. We are living beyond our means, and may continue to do so'.

Mr Stanley Baldwin (1933) 'And we all know that neither a nation nor an individual can go on forever living on borrowed money – a crash must inevitably come if such a policy is allowed to continue.'

Mr Ramsay Macdonald (1931) 'We are no longer exporting enough to pay for our necessary and very large imports of food and raw material. In a sentence . . .'

Mr Roy Jenkins (1968) '. . . our present economic situation is extremely serious.'

Mr Lloyd George (1931) 'The pound has collapsed!'

Mr Neville Chamberlain (1937) 'And it is that fact that has dominated this budget and not only made it impossible to reduce taxation, but rendered an increase of taxation inevitable.' *Pause.* 'This is a sad disappointment for me, as well as for you.'

Mr Hugh Dalton (1947) 'Clearly this can't go on!'

Mr Stanley Baldwin (1933) 'The country has decided, once and for all, that the budget *must be balanced* – whatever sacrifices are entailed.'

Mr Hugh Dalton (1947) 'Therefore, as I told the House of Commons today, we must reduce expenditure and we must increase taxation, unpleasant as this may be.'

Mr Rab Butler (1952) 'We mean to try to take a new line to get us out of our difficulties – the line of facing facts, of giving help where it is needed, and rewards for more work done.' *Pause.* 'Do you think this makes sense in our present situation?' *Long pause.*

God Bless the Prince of Wales

Mr Clement Attlee (1947) 'I have tried to set before you the facts of the situation because I know that if you're *told* the facts, and what must be done, you will respond.' *Pause*. 'The way out of our difficulties is *hard*.'

Mr Neville Chamberlain (1935) 'It will not be achieved in a day, or a month; but there are many willing hearts working at the problem, and I am convinced that by degrees we shall master it.'

Mr Stafford Cripps (1949) 'If we stick to it now, the time of full recovery will certainly come; and it's not the time now to falter, or hold back.'

Mr Hugh Dalton (1947) 'We shall need all our strength to overcome the difficulties ahead, but I am not disheartened: *we* are *Englishmen*!'

Mr Neville Chamberlain (1936) 'With care and prudence we may hope to bring our ship safely through into calmer waters.'

Mr N. Chamberlain (one year later) 'When the task has been completed, we shall be able to rest on our oars.' *Pause*.

NB Insidiously introduce an orchestral version of 'Land of Hope and Glory' and play quietly under.

Mr Rab Butler (1952) 'Our old country's got to be like that ship – taut and ready for anything. We *know* that we must reach the harbour safely. And that's why this budget braces you for an effort, and gives you a ray of hope.'

NB Crescendo 'Land of Hope and Glory', play to its conclusion and pause.

Announcer 'And that is the end of our Budget Special.' *Pause*. 'There now follows a short address by the Bishop of Walthamstow. His theme is: "Why I am still glad I'm British". . . .'

That suggestion was a conceit, a flight of fancy. Unfortunately the text was not. And although the extracts employed were garnered from speeches made during a thirty-seven year period ending in 1968, I guarantee that an avid researcher will reap an equally luxurious harvest of clichés from the rhetoric of more recent times. Fate, it seems, has ordained that we should always spit on our blistered hands and pull through a choppy sea for a far-off shore, as the pound sinks slowly in the west, and, as was the case in Carroll's 'Wonderland', there will never be jam today. Like the ubiquitous strike, it is part of our way of life; but it would be unfair to particularise on our crises and our shortcomings, and to ignore our successes.

Britain still has much to offer the outside world. Not all our achievements make banner headlines, but I well remember the pride which engulfed me when, in 1977 I opened a copy of the *Daily Telegraph* and read: 'BRITISH SUPER DUCKS GO TO WORK ON INDIAN EGG OUTPUT'.

It was an eyecatching caption: I read on. British ducks, I learned, lay 300 eggs a year compared with their Indian counterparts' ova rate of eighty. That in itself made pleasing reading. Even more heartwarming was the news that we, magnanimously and ever mindful of our responsibilities toward the peoples of our former empire, were to despatch 2,000 of our unsinkables to India on a mating spree. And I thought of another Drake who once kept England's flag a-flying. But, as I continued to read, what thrilled me hugely was the reassurance that the high standard of British diplomacy was still being maintained: these exported drakes were not to be just any odd randy Tom, Dick or Donald picked up in Regent's Park, but *Khaki* Campbells.

God Bless the Prince of Wales

It is not widely known, nor generally appreciated, the extent to which this demonstration of savoir faire played a part in influencing a better understanding between the two countries. Modesty is one of our national characteristics. We often fail to advertise our achievements, particularly those in the scientific field. In 1980, few, if any, foreign news agencies were advised of the diligence with which our scientists were addressing themselves to the problem of population control. Nor of their ingenuity. *Pravda* was unaware of the research; so was *Le Monde*; and *The Wall Street Journal*. Once again, it was left to the *Daily Telegraph* to blow a muted trumpet on our behalf, albeit on an inside page. 'SUPER GLUE FOR BIRTH CONTROL' they cried; and then elaborated:

Tests on a new, simple, method of birth control using a super glue have been carried out on volunteers at Bolton General Hospital. It is claimed to be quick and permanent but, a spokesman continued, there is still a long way to go before it is perfected.

I showed the paragraph to an American friend of mine, long resident in the north of the country, and well acquainted with the tenacity of the Lancastrian.

'Gee,' he said, and his eyes lingered over the last sentence. 'Knowing that lot, I bet they'll stick at it.' And he clicked his tongue admiringly.

He was right to do so. Mongrels though we be, we British are a splendid, and, as Sir Noël Coward once observed, a happy breed. However, we are also a funny breed; and in the eyes of the foreigner none are more peculiar than the English. As my late father would have said: 'You see my dear chap, they just don't understand us.' And he would have smiled, and sucked upon his pipe.

Now there *was* an Englishman . . . *par excellence*.

2

Relative Values

To be English (and proud of it) it is essential to be sired by
an indigenous parent no matter whether he originates
from the north, south, east or west of the country, and
ideally by a pipe-smoking one to boot.

The pipe is an invaluable accessory to any Englishman,
not so much for the stimulus afforded him by the tobacco
within, but because the filling and lighting of it, or even a
close examination of the bowl, allows him to gain time
while considering his reply to a question to which readily
he is unable to supply the answer. Indeed, with diligence
the experienced Briton may protract the proceedings to
such an extent that by the time he has blown out his Swan
Vesta his questioner may have forgotten the original
inquiry or, with luck, gone home. It is not mere
coincidence that Messrs Baldwin, Attlee and Wilson, all
scions from good English stock, were dedicated pipe-
smokers and among the best procrastinators in English
political life. To reiterate, the advantages of being
fathered by a briar-sucking Englishman are incalculable,
but with such a flying start in life one may look the world
and any immigration official squarely in the eye and with
an inherited and coverted arrogance, even if one's mother
is of foreign blood.

I was fortunate in both particulars. My father was the archetypal Englishman. Unless an introduction had been effected he never spoke to strangers, particularly foreigners whom instinctively he mistrusted; and when visiting the continent, which he did with extreme reluctance, he opened his mouth solely to remove his pipe or to admit food. This he disliked, on principle.

As a staunch Non-Conformist he feared both God and the Pope, albeit for different reasons; was deeply suspicious of Ivor Novello and men who wore after-shave lotion; conspicuously stood to attention during the playing of the National Anthem at the end of theatrical performances while all about him were rushing toward exits like demented lemmings; and always removed his hat when passing the Cenotaph. At a time when familiarity with the obelisk had robbed it of much of its emotional significance, this gesture did not pass unnoticed by younger men. However, no greater impact was made upon them than when, on an April day in 1961, his bowler left his head but its purple lining did not. Innocent of the fact, my father strode past the memorial to our glorious dead like a damson on stilts. He also retained his tie at all times regardless of climatic conditions; and never showed his braces. He was, as the French would say, 'très prôpre'.

Named William Ewart after the late Mr Gladstone by liberally-minded parents imbued, it would seem, with a bizarre sense of humour, my father had no political options open to him. Sartorially, however, he was implacably conservative. Only once did he pander to fashion. With grave misgivings but coerced by my mother, a personable woman with a continental upbringing and consequently a more avant-garde outlook

. . . and always removed his hat when passing the Cenotaph

on life, he replaced his fly buttons with a zip-fastener. However, following an unfortunate and harrowing experience in a public lavatory in Guildford to which he had repaired with indecent but necessary haste, and later vacated grey with pain and half an octave higher, he eschewed the latter, re-instated the former, and never adventured again.

His philosophy of life was refreshingly uncomplicated. Either one 'played the game' or one did not. Those who kept to the rules were gentlemen, regardless of their social status, and those who ignored them were cads or bounders. To those categories were admitted men who displayed propelling pencils or fountain pens in their top pockets, those who wore old school ties to which they were not entitled, and commissioned officers of the Home Guard and other irregular services who retained and used their rank in peace time. His objection to that practice was once made abundantly clear to an official of the Gas Light and Coke Company Ltd to such good effect that it was only with difficulty that the shamed and sometime Major was dissuaded from putting his head into one of his own ovens. But he did leave the district.

Equally beyond the pale were those who left their seats during overs at Lords or who gave tongue at Twickenham when conversions were being attempted. Such things were not done, which is why I am glad that my father is no longer with us, for nowadays they are; and sport is the poorer for both gestures. Nor would he have approved of the current trend of denigrating one's own country, for whilst privily he was not averse to voicing uncharitable thoughts about the efficiency of the Cabinet or even, God save the mark, that of the MCC, he would never proclaim his reservations in public. That too was not done. Lastly, such lies as he did tell were always white ones. As my mother once observed to me: 'Your father is a very good man.' And she sighed, wistfully.

My mother was a beautiful woman from the French-speaking part of Switzerland, a Genevoise, tall and elegant with deep brown eyes and shapely ankles and blessed with a wicked tongue and the ability to dress well on a limited budget. By contrast my father was blue-eyed, short and stocky and managed without effort to give the impression that he had slept in his clothes during a long period of hibernation; but despite a trenchant wit, and unlike my mother, he was never calculatingly hurtful with words.

In his own unemotional way he adored her. From time to time he even remembered her name; but he never displayed his feelings toward her publicly. What happened in the privacy of their bedroom was something about which I often conjectured when I reached puberty, but after much deliberation and some evidence I came to the conclusion that sex had little appeal to my father. His moments of ecstasy and euphoria, I determined, were not excited and furnished by women, but by the sight of a well executed cover drive or the sound of a scrum-half in extremis. Only once did I broach him on the subject.

At the age of fourteen-and-a-half and unbelievably innocent of any of the physical facts of life, despite having had my right knee caressed by an ageing homosexual sergeant-major of my school's OTC while returning by train from a field-day in Shebbear, I advised him that I was experiencing a certain early morning stiffness in a private part of my body. Uneasily he digested the intelligence, turned a deep shade of magenta and pulled at his moustache. 'Ah,' he said, and coughed several times before leading me into the bathroom. 'Personally', he continued, coming to a halt before the wash-basin and lowering his voice as if about to deliver the Lord's Prayer 'when that happens to *me*, I stick it under the cold tap.'

My acne worsened visibly. Moreover, not only did the advice shock my nervous system and arrest my natural development for several months, but from that moment I entertained a near paranoid dislike of cold water of any kind. It was also one of the few parental recommendations to fall on stony ground. However, in other respects my father was a splendid mentor.

He taught me how to gather and pass a rugby ball when I was seven, advised me that only soccer players or dagos made a fuss when they were kicked, and at the same age instructed me how to hold a cricket bat. He applauded me roundly when I broke two scullery windows in quick succession off his under-arm deliveries with a soft ball, mollified our general factotum who was working at the sink at the time by bribing her with a shilling; and by spanking me soundly for kicking my wicket in a fit of pique he instilled in me the importance of accepting an umpire's decision at all times, and of being a good loser. As I was seldom allowed the luxury of being a good winner this advice was to prove invaluable to me. Particularly during the war. 'Never mind,' I mused while swinging below the flapping canopy of a parachute and watching the riddled remains of my aeroplane spiralling earthward toward alien territory, 'they'll know a good loser when they see one, they'll do the decent thing.' Unfortunately, and as was made quite clear to me upon my arrival on terra firma, my hosts were unaware of the maxim. But as my

46

father said later: 'My dear chap, what can you expect from foreigners?'

Although, unlike the late General Montgomery, my father never referred to God as 'that Great Umpire in the Sky' or prayed that he be allowed to 'hit the enemy for six', much of his vocabulary was made up of sporting metaphors. Shortly before he died, unpleasantly but with a quiet dignity from cancer, in a cottage hospital, I visited him and looked with sadness at the yellowing echo of the man who had authored me. His eyes were still blue but rheumy with age and illness and his pipe lay untouched and unwanted in a glass ash-tray beside his bed.

I stayed for a while, holding his hand and talking quietly in a desultory fashion about trivialities until he closed his eyes and dozed, and in his half sleep returned to the Somme and Flanders fields and mumbled the name of his younger brother who had fallen as others had done in bloodied heaps at Menin, in the war to end all wars. And he called upon his father and the King and cried out for stretcher-bearers, and spoke the names of Larwood and of Chamberlain. And so I waited with him as the spectres of half a century flitted through his muddled mind, and the gold half-hunter on his bedside table ticked away the minutes of his life.

It was when I disengaged my hand and eased myself from his bed that he reawakened. I said softly: 'I think it's time I went now. But I'll see you tomorrow, if that's all right?' The blue eyes looked hazily but directly at me under half-lowered lids. 'Yes,' he said, 'yes. Of course. But I think it's time I was getting back to the pavilion too.' He gave a little sigh like that of a tired child at the end of a long day. 'After all,' he said, 'I've been at the crease for quite a while you know . . . quite a while . . . I've had a very good innings.' And gently turning his head away, he smiled into the pillow.

Later that evening I was told that he had died and for a long while I mourned his passing, for with his death, or so it seemed to me, a little Englishness had been irretrievably lost and a little greenness had gone from the land. But I was wrong. My father's generation may be clay but many of his qualities and those of his contemporaries are manifest in their heirs. Men of their calibre are still to be found in the cities, villages and country towns of England; and without them many a church would be found wanting for wardens and many a voluntary organisation short of staff. Not all are retired soldiers and sailors, but all give service to their communities as they go about their businesses, unpaid and unpraised. These are they at whom it is fashionable for present adolescents to poke fun; to brand them as antiquated survivors of a past society. And they in turn, forgetting the enormities of their own youth which threatened to turn their fathers prematurely bald, look askance at the younger generation and raising their eyes toward the heavens ask if there's hope for England.

'Our youth', cried one such apoplectic, 'has bad manners, disregards authority and has no respect whatsoever for age; today's children are tyrants; they do not get up when an elderly man enters the room; they talk back to their parents; they are just, very bad.'
His name was Socrates.

Socrates was a Greek. But regardless of nationality, his sentiments have been, and will be, endorsed throughout the ages. And as future generations come and go, the same cry will go up from Land's End to John O'Groats; for that is the way of the world. Mercifully, however, and possibly as a result of Divine Intervention, our heritage and traits miraculously are preserved. But this should come as no surprise. As every true Briton knows in his heart of hearts, and as my father frequently inferred, God *is* an Englishman.

In retrospect I owe much to my father. By profession he was a soldier, a field officer in an unfashionable but distinguished regiment of foot. However, despite that handicap, he was remarkably articulate and well read. On the other hand he was not particularly sympathetic toward the arts in general.

Musically he was uneducated and disinterested in the subject, and although the owner of a pleasant baritone voice the only songs I ever heard him sing were, 'Keep the Home Fires Burning', and a well-tried selection from the works of Moody and Sankey. These he delivered with great power and a total neglect of phrasing either from the carbolic-scented waters of his bath or whilst ensconced upon the lavatory. Opera was anathema to him, largely because most of the performers were foreigners, and he once snored loudly through a rendering of 'Your Tiny Hand is Frozen' causing the Rudolpho of the time to go off key and affording acute embarrassment to my mother who had bullied him first into evening dress, and then through the doors of Covent Garden. She never repeated the experiment. Nor was he drawn toward the theatre although, excluding the sonnets, he entertained a high regard for the works of Shakespeare.

Henry V was his favourite. The fact that the play distorted or ignored historical truths and glossed over the

EE-D

49

less attractive characteristics of the king was of as little consequence to him as it had been to Shakespeare; Harry was shown as a thoroughly decent God-fearing chap and the French were portrayed as pimps, ponces and blackguards; and that was as it should be. But his admiration of English literature was boundless and his library, though small, was comprehensive.

He cared for books, not only for their literary merits but for the craftsmanship which had made them and would run his hand over their calf leather covers and caress the patina which the years had gathered, or take them to his nose and smell the pot-pourri of print and polish as a gardener does a rose; and he transmitted his enjoyment of them to me.

Enthusiastically he directed me toward finely-tooled volumes of Dickens and Thackeray and Kipling and Swift, introduced me to cloth-covered copies of Priestley and Moreton and Wodehouse and 'Saki', and told me that Shaw was agnostic and Wilde was worse. Nevertheless he allowed that although Irish, both men wrote beautiful English and should be read unreservedly. After his death I was given further proof of the catholicity of his reading.

I discovered a faded blue book dedicated in 1910 to the then Bishop of Carlisle improbably entitled *A Thousand Things to Say in Sermons* containing among other textual gems one reading 'Whenever a Sheep bleats it loses a Mouthful', against which a grateful incumbent had pencilled the marginal 'used Evensong, Godalming Parish Church, February 1910'; a paperback on *How to Enjoy Your Budgerigar* which I believed to be a compendium of exotic recipes; and a splendidly illustrated tome on the history of the briar pipe.

Relative Values

The last named came as no surprise to me. My father was an authority on pipes; indeed I suspect that he had emerged from the womb with this insignia of the true Englishman clasped between his toothless gums. Understandably therefore, it was to him I turned for advice when, in my seventeenth year, I acquired my first pipe.

It was a cherry wood, thick and rustic with a wooden stem and mouthpiece and, as I was to discover later, a very thin base. It cost fourpence ha'penny and I bought it together with some tobacco inappositely named Nosegay during the school holidays in 1939. For two weeks I smoked it vigorously but surreptitiously before facing him with the news that I had become a man.

My father was a stern man but a fair one and, no doubt recalling his own cloaked initiation, he received my confession sympathetically and with only a modicum of surprise at my honesty. Together we sat in his study, and as he began filling his pipe, I lit mine. Quickly the atmosphere polluted. My father stiffened in his chair, leaned forward and sniffed inquiringly like a disbelieving bloodhound. 'I don't know what you're smoking,' he said, 'but whatever it is it's not an officer's tobacco.'

Involuntarily I inhaled and looked at him with streaming eyes. 'It's called Nosegay,' I said. My father raised his eyebrows. 'Really?' he said, 'Is it *really*.' Ten seconds later a hot plug of tobacco attended by a shower of wood ash and sparks fell from the bottom of the cherry wood and burned a hole in the Axminster. Momentarily my father gazed at it in silence. 'And', he added with remarkable self control, 'I don't think that's much of a pipe either.'

51

Relative Values

Not only was my father a master of the understatement he was, as I found out over the years, correct on both counts. There *are* tobaccos which one lets off rather than smokes; and there are pipes which become funeral pyres within a comparatively short while and upon which one is tempted to commit sutti; and those from which stoppings of putty fall like hailstones after only a few bowlfuls. With experience, the discerning Englishman desirous of keeping friends and reaching old age learns to avoid both.

As often as not these products are purchased by the unwary or uncaring, of which I was one, from suburban or country shops bearing the legend 'Tobacconists, Confectioners and Newsagents'. These sell popular brands of cigarettes and tobaccos, boiled sweets and sun-bleached pipes, plastic snowstorms depicting scenes of stoic frost-bitten Guardsmen outside Buckingham Palace, and occasionally contraceptives. Sometimes the proprietors' hedge their bets by stocking birth congratulatory cards as well but all their wares are displayed in south-facing windows with a cavalier disregard for the finer points of merchandising, and no English scene would be complete without them.

In such establishments one is served either by large middle-aged ladies who call you 'dear', or totally resistible young ones who don't call you anything. Invariably the latter, adjusting an errant brassière strap the while, address themselves to an imaginary spot above one's right shoulder and say 'yerse?' Secretly they hate you for having disturbed them and wish you to go away; but neither type knows anything about pipes.

It was against such places that my father advised me to turn my back, and by so doing opened up a part of London which hitherto had been unknown to me. 'Come!' he commanded one bright August morning, and escorted me to the West End of the city. Gently he led me into the environs of Pall Mall and St James, lunched me frugally at the Army and Navy, and piloted me unrepleted but impressed through the prodigious respectability of Club Land. Past the awesome Athenacum, spilling out begaitered bishops, purple-clothed and purple-faced slow-moving galleons of the Church, round and heavy with steak and kidney; past the Reform and Brooks's and Boodles; and into the equally rarified atmosphere of Jermyn and Duke Streets. There lay the pipeman's Mecca, the happy hunting ground of the cognoscenti. On all sides I saw men from whose expensive faces drooped or protruded expensive briars, who moved in a refined aura of latakia or rich Virginia, men who had never known Nosegay and for whom shag was a vulgar expression. All wore bowler hats, white collars and striped shirts, and all carried furled umbrellas which they swung with panache in the late summer sun.

I watched them emerging from premises like Charatan's, pipe-makers since 1863, peering into the antique amber and meerschaum filled windows of Astleys, or genuflecting as they passed through the portals of Dunhill's. My father led me into each in turn and in each I was enlightened on the art and craft of English pipe-making and smoking. That was the year before bombs from fat Goering's Heinkels came and blew their shop fronts on to the elegant pavements; when sales staff looked upon their customers not as interrupting nuisances but greeted them with courtesy and care. Discontented they may have been with life, but unlike many of their modern counterparts in darkest Lewisham or Penge they hid their ennui and were never rude gratuitously. They were the professionals for whom the word service was not a class-orientated anachronism equated with servility, but who aimed to please.

'Perhaps, sir,' they murmured, dark-suited and discreetly over the clatter of a client's outraged dentures, 'perhaps the Large Rhodesian *is* a trifle heavy. May we suggest a Medium Apple? Or a Billiard? Or even, perchance, a Liverpool Shell with, ahem! a fish-tail mouthpiece?' It was into emporia like those that a man could stride urgently crying, 'I want a Large Pot!' and be confident that none would think him incontinent.

Dunhill's was one such establishment. Within it pin-striped trousered acolytes wearing grey silk ties handled their wares with white cotton gloves and spoke of them with reverence. As English as the roast beef of Simpson's, that paradise of carnivors in the Strand, its retinue left no stone unturned to help their patrons choose wisely. Disposable mouth clips were fitted to stems so that balance and bite could be tested on site; mirrors revealed what face and pipe looked like when assembled, and advice was offered on shape and suitability. Not all, alas, accepted it. Small men could be seen staggering into Duke Street with giant pipes clamped in their tiny jaws. Veins stood out from their foreheads as they walked with popping eye-balls as if in the teeth of a gale, destined to go through life at a permanent angle of forty-five degrees. Doubtless they returned home to large bullying wives who banished them to smoke in isolation in ordure-smelling garden sheds, but their egos were satisfied. *And*, for the price of 25 shillings, they possessed a Dunhill – a white-spotted, prestige symbol of their material success through which they puffed their superiority. Many a social unfortunate of the time, obliged by force of circumstance to suck upon a lesser briar, lowered his eyes when a Dunhill man went by.

I often think back to those late school, pre-Royal Air Force days of my adolescence when the war clouds lowered over Europe and eventually put out the lights of London; and whenever I walk those West End streets today the ghost of my father goes with me. Despite having little in common with him aesthetically, I admired him greatly and saw in him many of the qualities attributed to St Paul. Particularly when it came to the subject of food and wine.

The Apostle Paul, who, it will be remembered, once dictated a terse letter to the Corinthians suggesting that they went easy on the retsina and another to Timothy also urging moderation for his stomach's sake, clearly was not a bon viveur. Neither was my father. With regard to victuals, and with the proviso that whatever was put upon his plate included a liberal helping of potatoes and did not move, unblinkingly he ate anything that was put before him. On the matter of wine he was less discerning and consequently unable to offer me tutelage in that province. However, fortunately for me, this disastrous flaw in my education was redressed under the aegis of another splendid Englishman – my wicked Uncle Chris.

Educated at Blundell's, from which he parted company without distinction save that of shouting 'down with this Popery', and causing a Downside boy to be carried unconscious from the rugby field in 1919, plus the proven ability to drain north Devon of rough cider, wicked Uncle

Chris was the antithesis of my father. Wicked Uncle Chris had nothing in common with St Paul. On the other hand it is equally true to affirm that he did have a marked affinity with Winnie the Pooh. Invariably, long words did puzzle him; he did have a useful box for putting things in; and, without being uncharitable, his brain was a little on the small side. He also addressed everyone, regardless of sex, as 'Old fruit', or 'Cock'; but he had immense charm and Wodehouse would have embraced him.

Family historians relate that upon leaving school the year following his physical encounter with the Catholic lock-forward at Tiverton, he devoted himself exclusively to perfecting the intricate steps of the Black Bottom and the Bunny Hug, and to the execution of the Charleston. Inevitably such wholehearted dedication brought him in contact with divers Bright Young Women, none of whom my father would have entertained in his drawing room. Fleetingly, all of them entered his life comparatively empty-handed, and all accelerated from it considerably enriched, if not ennobled. Wicked Uncle Chris could never say 'no', and when tutorially he entered my life the two-way traffic was still continuing and showing no sign of abatement.

Unlike my father, who when out of uniform caused many to believe that his mission in life was to scare off birds, my uncle was the epitome of the well-dressed man-about-town. His hair, dark and Brylcreemed and parted in the centre, was cut at Trumpers, his suits were tailored in Savile Row, and he always carried an unblemished white handkerchief in his left-hand sleeve. He rallied to Monte Carlo, drove at Brooklands and skied at Gstaad; he played lawn tennis adequately and club rugby well; and he could

. . . Wodehouse would have embraced him

belch through the alphabet unhesitatingly from A to Z, and quell a Head Waiter in five seconds flat. In short, he was a well-rounded fellow, a son of whom England justly can be proud, and in the period between my leaving school and learning to fight in the air, I became indebted to him and placed him on a pedestal. Uncle Chris admitted me to one of the great secrets of life. He taught me how to mix a dry martini.

As a maker of dry martinis, my uncle had no equal.

His knowledge of gin and its employment was prodigious. To concoct a martini with anything but Beefeater or Tanqueray was, he advised me, tantamount to blasphemy; and to make a Pink Gin and not use Plymouth's was unthinkable. As for other distillations from Booth's and Gordon's these, he assured me, should be reserved only for use with tonic waters and he once brought a barman at the Café Royal close to tears for doing otherwise. It was not for nothing that he had removed a replica of Holman Hunt's *Light of the World* from above his bed head where it shared pride of place with a photograph of the Saracens' 'A' rugby football team and replaced it with a framed copy of an A. P. Herbert eulogy, 'In Praise of the Juniper'. Wicked Uncle Chris liked his gin. However, his erudition in the field of alcohol was by no means confined to the spirit world. He was equally *au fait* with the end products from the vineyards of Bordeaux and Burgundy, not to mention those of the Rhône and Alsace. And he enjoyed more than a nodding acquaintance with the hop-gardens of Kent.

He demonstrated this truth to me with avuncular enthusiasm. Within the space of eight months he introduced me to the saloon and private bars of every reputable public house in the capital, one or two disreputable ones on its periphery, and together we drank our way through London from Ward's Irish Bar in Piccadilly to the Spaniards' Inn at Hampstead. I tasted beer from Charrington's, Watney's and Bass, brown ale, light ale and black and tan, bitter and mild beers straight from the wood, Younger's and Theakston's in free houses; and learned how to pour a Worthington. It was a joyous apprenticeship and only on one occasion did an excursion end in disaster. On a cold January night in 1941, and as the German bombers droned overhead, I was sick on my uncle's carpet slippers. Characteristically, and despite them being new, he bore me no grudge but saved my face by attributing the outrage to a mixture of indifferent bitter, inclement weather, and the bombing. To reiterate, he was a fine Englishman.

Patently my uncle knew his beers; but his forté was with wines, and this expertise was also passed to me and included in my crash course of hedonism, despite the attendant discomforts of war brought to us from the air. Delicately, like sore-footed chickens, we scrunched over broken glass and picked our way to 43 Pall Mall, home of Christopher & Co Ltd, wine merchants since 1666 and supplier to the king; thence to Justerini and Brooks at Number Two, from whom His Majesty also bought the occasional bottle of Médoc, and on to Berry Bros & Rudd in St James' Street. They too collected their empties from the Palace. Miraculously, all had escaped the close attentions of the Luftwaffe and in each my uncle was persona grata and was proffered a glass of Madeira and a Bath Oliver. And so was I. It was all most civilised, and English.

I learned a great deal as I sipped and listened to these polymaths of port and burgundy as they talked of age and elegance, of balanced acidity, and Beaujolais and Beaune. These were the experts, Englishmen who had been weaned on wine and cut their teeth on claret; zealots who had sniffed and swilled and spat their ways through the years, who dreamily trod grapes by night and drank the juice by day, and I was glad when I heard them rejoice that 1940 had been a rotten year for burgundy and no more than the occupying Huns deserved. But they shook their heads when the talk turned to the future. In England, in 1941, it was not wise to think too far ahead.

At the time, those savants to whom I listened seemed as old as Dionysius, but on reflection they were probably in their early forties or otherwise deemed unfit for military service. By now, all must be tending vines in Elysium fields, but during the blitz the doors of their establishments never closed, and they were still open when I returned from the war wounded by NAAFI beer and thirsty for wine and further education. And they are still in business, albeit in other premises. All except Berry Bros & Rudd. They have remained *in situ* near St James' Palace.

The offices of the Brothers Berry are very old. They are dim and spacious and have bare wooden floors and I have a conceit that after hours French chalk is scattered upon them, a portable gramophone wound up and that the staff of four enjoin in a minuet behind closed dusty doors; Berry Bros & Rudd are a decorous firm. Moreover, they have retained what a great-aunt of mine would have described as carriage trade and an old world ambience. Certainly I would hesitate to cross their threshold wearing bicycle clips and in search of half a bottle of house claret. However, if I did so, I should be received graciously, as I would be in Christopher's, or Justerini and Brooks. What is more, I should be provided with a carrier bag. Free. In that respect, nothing has altered since 1941. The mannerly successors to those pundits of the past continue the tradition of expert service; but other aspects of English life have changed. And not only the quality of the carriage trade.

Forty-four years ago, wine drinking was the prerogative of a privileged minority. Now, happily for the EEC and the Chancellor of the Exchequer, a high proportion of Englishmen and women from all walks of life have discovered the inestimable joy of looking through a glass darkly. Consequently, wine shops of many kinds have sprung up throughout the length and breadth of England. Unfortunately, not all the incumbents are blessed with a knowledge of what is in their bottles. Moreover, many do not care, appearing to have gained their employment solely on an ability to determine the colour red from white.

Employees of such concerns where external notices are often displayed in multi-coloured chalks exhorting passers-by to taste the bottled sunshine of Spain, embrace the Pauline philosophy that a *little* wine is good for the stomach. 'Indeed', they reason, momentarily unmindful of the Apostle's caveat as they eye their cash registers, 'a *lot* of wine is good for the stomach.' But like St Paul, who might well have added 'any old wine' and never once advised his readers to avoid 'that precocious little Macedonian '34' or directed them toward the Tuscany 1BC with the addendum 'roguish but will keep', they lack discernment and expertise. Manifestly St Paul was not a wine buff. He could not, for example, have advised one on what to drink with a well-hung grouse. And nor can they. I know. I asked one.

It was an unhappy moment in his life. 'Er,' he said, moistening his lips with his tongue and showing other signs of strain. 'Er, wadermin'.' And disappeared through a curtain to the rear of the shop. Minutes later he was replaced by a brisker colleague smelling strongly of down-market eau de Cologne.

'Yes?' said the scented one brightly, hitching his trousers and clapping his hands together, 'What's the problem, squire?' I repeated the question.

'Ah yes,' he said, 'yes. The old grouse ay?', and gestured toward a wicker basket labelled 'Special Offer'. 'These', he said, 'are very popular. These go very well these do. Yes,' he added giving himself an encore, 'we sell a lot of these we do. Oh yes.'

I left him standing behind a window filled with assorted bottles of vins de table resting cheek by jowl with Pernod and vodka and balanced upon rows of lager tins. All were coming nicely to blood heat in the full sun. He was a nice lad selling, as all employees at such places do, tolerable plonk at reasonable prices; but he did not imbue me with confidence. Not as they do at Berry Bros & Rudd or Christopher's where they salivate at the thought of well-hung grouse and cross themselves at the mention of a Margaux '45. Further, there they do not call one squire; and they never will. These are today's Yesterday's Men – impeccably conservative in dress and manner who will, in turn, give way to tomorrow's Men of Yesterday.

Much has happened to England and the English since Flannagan and Allen sang 'Run Rabbit Run' and prematurely advised us that 'ere long we should 'Hang Out the Washing on the Siegfried Line'. We have won a war and lost an empire; watched our cities grow phoenix-like and high-rise from their ashes, and seen the scars of London healed by architectural cosmeticism. We have said goodbye to the penny and accepted new pence and resisted the metre, the litre and kilo. We have seen women admitted to the Stock Exchange, girls to the sixth forms of our public schools, and other changes too bizarre to mention; and we have fought bravely, but vainly, against the phasing out of Fahrenheit. But one thing we have not lost: an awareness of our social divisions. Rutherford may have split the atom, but the English class structure remains intact, as many layered as a mille-feuille pastry.

There is no escaping from that truth. All of us live within one stratum or another of the cake, easily recognisable to others by sight, behaviour and sound. Especially sound. As soon as an Englishman opens his mouth he betrays the tier to which he belongs. He even reveals when he's in oral transit. But despite what modern sociologists tell us, this is no bad thing. Accent and class are the causes for much of the humour in our everyday lives. And the one thing the English do superlatively well is to laugh at each other, and themselves. It is one of our ethnic strengths. And perhaps that is why we survive in a sometimes humourless world, entirely surrounded by foreigners.

The English puzzle foreigners; and with good reason. As a bemused Austrian lady once observed to me: 'What can you make of people who say "sorry" and "thank you" to the dog?'

We even flummox the Greeks.

3

She-pard's Boosh

'Ah Yanni!' rhapsodied an anglophile Greek friend of
mine on the island of Andros and who, despite never
having been to England, had a remarkable knowledge of
English, 'She-pard's Boosh! That, for my opinion, is the
place most up my passage as you might say. Ah yes,' he
enlarged, leaning back in his chair and continuing to
eulogise with half closed eyes, 'it fills me with love this
words, She-pard's Boosh! So many sheep I think, so many
green, green fields, so much boosh. And all, so so
proximus to London as you might say from the maps.
She-pard's Boosh!' He repeated the name, savouring it
like a mouthful of moussaka, and looked at me for
confirmation. 'You know it Yanni? This She-pard's
Boosh?' 'Yes', I said, thinking of another foreign friend
who entertained similar misconceptions about the
blackened brick and concrete blasphemy of London
Fields, 'I do. Very well.' And destroyed his romantic
imagery as kindly as I could.

Doubtless at one time cows did chew the cud in London
Fields and sheep did gambol near the Goldhawk Road. No
doubt in ages past the air was heady with the fragrance of
flowers, and shepherds called to shepherdesses and
invited them to be their loves; but not now. Now the only

sheep one sees in Shepherd's Bush are nocturnal ones and mostly dressed as lamb, and the scents are those of the brewery and the diesel lorry, of onions frying in vegetable oil; and fish and chips and curry; and the language of courtship which peaks in the small hours of grey mornings is more urgent and prosaic than that of Marlowe. I know. Circumstances once dictated that I should leave the cloistered comfort of a country village and live in Shepherd's Bush.

I arrived in the area one Shrove Tuesday evening and left it two years later. It was the most exacting and prolonged Lenten penance I have ever experienced; but it was a salutory period. In Shepherd's Bush I discovered how the other half lives and, as a man suddenly bereft of sight lives on the memories of nature's beauty, so did I. Occasionally I glimpsed a dew-bejewelled spider's web hanging between rusting iron railings, or the iridescence on a preening starling's wing, and once on a moonless night I saw Orion and the Dog Star Sirius coruscating and hanging in a winter's sky as I walked along the crowded, litter-strewn pavements of the Uxbridge Road. But such moments were rare, and I learned to hoard them.

The two rooms in which I lived were at the top of a three-storeyed Victorian house in Loftus Road. Like most of the property in the immediate neighbourhood it had known better days. Much better days. Within seventy-two hours of my taking residence I was all but guillotined by a rotting window frame as I searched for what cynically, in that region, passed for air, and a week later a sampler advising me that God is Love, and bearing with it an ample lump of wall plaster, fell on my head. A moderate shower produced drips through the ceiling and anything more substantial, near monsoon conditions. Shortly after each occurrence, a middle-aged and foul-mouthed incompetent named Lancaster would appear on the landing with an unstable ladder and a large hammer and vanish through an overhead trapdoor. Within the abyss beyond, to where none but the very brave or foolhardy ventured, he would bang and blaspheme for several minutes before reappearing with a heightened colour and an enlarged thumb. The rain continued to come through the ceiling.

Adjoining my bedroom was the communal bathroom. Decoratively, it enjoyed a similar state of repair as the rest of the house. Unheated and unloved, it contained a cracked hand basin over which was mounted an example of one of the earlier types of geyser and upon which was emblazoned the misleading legend 'Reliant'. Resting upon a warped unpainted shelf constructed of six-ply, its laminae long since steamed apart, and surrounded by an ever-rising hillock of spent matches, this survivor from the age of Ramsay Macdonald ineffectively fed a monstrous brown stained bath of an even earlier period and capable of admitting not one, but several bathers, simultaneously. I seldom used it. But the Man From The Room Below did.

To the Man From The Room Below, that bath was his second home. To him it was not merely a place for lavation but a shrine – he all but slept in it. Daily, as the first shafts of sunlight kissed the slated roofs of Shepherd's Bush and on his return in the evening, he would bound from his room and up the stairs, bespectacled and sometimes naked, but always armed with a bottle of bath essence and a giant sponge, and incarcerate himself within his temple. And there he would stay for an hour or more, never singing, but moaning softly in aquatic ecstasy. What unseen pleasures he afforded himself during his total immersion were never made known to me, but I suspected he did dreadful things with a loofah. I named him Orca.

Orca co-habited with a voluptuous lady of generous proportions whose origins were from the Middle or Near East and whose livelihood was the marketing of perfumes and unguents from the same quarter of the globe. That she was dedicated to the advertising of her products was beyond question. One was always aware of her presence. By the same token I knew that both she and her amphibious consort shared an enthusiasm for do-it-yourself paella on Thursdays, and instant curry on the Sabbath. Beyond that I was in receipt of no other personal details about them. We moved to each other when passing on the stairs or whilst uneasily awaiting admittance to a single lavatory on the ground floor, but otherwise we behaved impeccably and ignored each other as behoves mannerly English people who had never been introduced.

The lavatory, an uninviting cubicle permanently occupied by a geriatric spider which eked out a precarious existence in a cobwebbed corner above the rusting cistern, was adjacent to a double bedroom shared by my landladies. This in turn was next to their front parlour used only by the two of them on Sundays, or if they had company. In the interim period they lived in a cluttered basement room together with nine cats of doubtful parentage and even more dubious habits. I first set foot in it when making my initial monthly payment of rent, and left it quickly, determined to meet my future commitments by standing order. It was very close in that

She-pard's Boosh

room.

My landladies were as different as chalk from cheese. Rejoicing respectively in the diminutives of Eff and Ange, and both in their middle sixties, the former was obese and indolent, while Ange was angular and active. She was also very kind. She laughed readily and raucously at life in general, and herself in particular. By contrast, Eff was a thin-lipped, uncharitable woman, mean of mouth and amused by nothing, whose entertainment was to spy on others and report on their activities, actual or imaginary. Daily she would take herself into the parlour where, big buttocked and bosomed, she would curl herself on a sofa by the window and there, like a bloated black widow in its web, peer through an uplifted corner of the net curtaining and unblinkingly watch the world go by. Nothing escaped her. However, Eff and Ange shared three particulars. Either of them would have made the Medusa appear as a raving beauty; each entertained a lively and thinly veiled hostility toward the other; and both had a mutual love of cats.

Neither Eff nor Ange could resist cats. No stray, however unpleasing in appearance or mentally disturbed, was ever refused succour, or turned away from the doors; the place was a feline doss-house. Cats were omnipresent. One-eared Toms in transit peered malevolently through the banister rails or crouched like coiled springs in darkened corners; ginger ones with half a tail, and squinting with anxiety, peeped out suspiciously from behind the hat-stand in the hall, and black ones could be seen sitting with half-closed eyes on the tops of the paraffin convectors, warming their bottoms and deep in horrid thought. And under the cover of darkness they met and did

68

objectionable things to each other. Next morning, temporarily satisfied and refreshed, most would leave and make their way back to the much-loved dustbins and alleyways of Shepherd's Bush. But not all. Some would remain and swell the ranks of the permanent residents.

One such cat was Roger.

Roger was one of the world's unfortunates. At times even the other cats were hard pressed to accept him socially. Roger's kidneys were not all that a tom cat's kidneys should be; evidence of his occupation was manifest long before one entered the house. Indeed, visiting postmen were known to blanch and stagger as they learned of Roger's incumbency via the letter box. But Roger was much loved by Eff and Ange. He was the cankered apple of their eye. And it was through Roger that I was invited into the parlour.

Prior to my removal to Shepherd's Bush, my Monday archival offerings on Radio 4 featured my Siamese cat, Perseus, whose personal and often stringent observations of life and contemporary notabilities were reported by me and, as hearsay, were free from accusations of slander. His fan mail easily eclipsed my own. When he died his passing was mentioned on a national news bulletin, and in the midday edition of the *London Evening Standard*. Consequently, not only did I bask in the reflected glory and erudition of Perseus, but I gained an erroneous reputation for being an authority on the behaviour of cats. Spurious though it was, it was that standing which brought Ange to the door of my bedsitter on a Sabbath afternoon.

'Ah Mr Eb, er Hebingdon,' she said, illustrating her life-long and losing battle with the placing of aspirates, 'ay wonder if you can 'elp, er help?' 'Well,' I said, 'I will if I can. Come in. Now then,' I said encouragingly, as she perched herself primly on the edge of the bed, 'what's the trouble?'

'Well,' she said, continuing to confirm that at some time in the past she had embarked upon a course of elocution lessons and had been told that it was common to elide, 'Ay do not know, reely. That is the trouble you see. Yes. Ay do not know. No. And nor does my friend, Eff. She do not know naither. No. But it is Roger, Mr Hebingdon. Our cat. Ay think you know him, do you not? Our cat? Roger?'

'Oh yes,' I said, 'at least, I know of him.' 'Yes,' said Ange, 'yes you would. He is all over the place Roger is. Yes. And he is a lovely pussy Mr Hebingdon, a lovely pussy but', and here she paused, 'he do 'ave a small problem. Yes.'

'Yes,' I said, marvelling at her understatement, 'I thought he might.' Ange paused again. 'You know what I mean?' she said.

I nodded.

'He pongs', said Ange.

'Yes.'

'A lot.'

'I had noticed.'

'And he is getting worse.'

'Oh dear.'

'Peter spat at him yesterday.'

'Tch! Tch!'

'And so did Claude. And Bruce. Claude stuck his claws in, Claude did. In his 'ead – er, head. And that', said Ange, bringing the catalogue of justifiable revenge to a close, 'is

70

why I am here. Could you', she asked, 'have a look at Roger – a good look that is? You know, close? You see,' she concluded, 'we know you love pussies. On the wireless.'

There was a short silence. 'He is in the front room', she said. 'With Eff.'

I took a deep breath. 'I'd be delighted to,' I said. And followed her down the stairs, and into the parlour.

The poet Keats, whose well-documented fondness for mellow fruitfulness and other manifestations of the turn of the year is legendary, would have approved of Eff and Ange's front room. True, he would have had to have settled for an opened bottle of Mackeson's stout in place of a cider press, but in all other respects he would have felt at home. The whole room reflected the seasonal tints of autumn. The wall-to-wall carpeting was of rust, the three-piece suite, fringed and huge and draylon-covered, was in gold, long curtains in similar material were of an arresting orange; the tone poem was continued by an oriental vase containing a dried bunch of Chinese lanterns upon a neon-lighted glass-fronted sideboard, and on the walls a skein of porcelain geese flew chipped and uncertainly across an avalanche of falling autumn leaves. The human interest was provided by Eff, overflowing from an armchair and clasping a tumbler of stout; and Roger. Curled before a spluttering gas fire burning at full throttle and on dampening layers of opened copies of the *News of the World* and other papers, he was not the happiest of cats.

'Well! Well! Well!' I said, trying hard to convey sympathy, but grateful that a head cold blunted one of my senses, 'poor old Roger! Poor old chap! What's the matter then, eh?'

'He leaks,' said Eff, taking a sip at her stout, 'that's

71

'He pongs, Mr Hebingdon'

what he does – leaks.'

'Yes,' I said, watching a page of the *People* slowly change colour before my eyes, 'he does seem to, doesn't he? Just a little, that is. But tell me', I said, mindful of my mission and fame as cat doctor extraordinaire, 'does he, er – urinate all the time?'

Eff sniffed disdainfully and tossed her head. 'I don't know about no unirations', she snapped, 'but he's pissed on the curtains.' '*And*', endorsed Ange, simultaneously raising the level of reportage, 'yesterday he toileted himself on the chair.'

She looked at me imploringly. 'What is the matter with him Mr Hebingdon? What should we do?'

'Well', I said, 'quite honestly I think you should take him to the vet.' 'Huh!' snorted Eff, 'that ponce? Doesn't know his arse from his elbow, he doesn't.' 'Possibly', I said, 'but he may know about Roger's kidneys.' 'Yes!' said Ange on a rising cadence and stamping her foot, 'of course he does! You are quite right Mr Hebingdon, quite right! We will take him to the cat hospital tomorrow – first thing we will. Yes! And *you*', she shrilled at Eff and momentarily stripped of her gentility, 'can shut yer face!' She turned to me. 'Would you care, Mr Hebingdon', she inquired sweetly, 'to partake of a glass of stout?'

They did take Roger to the vet. The next afternoon a taxi called for them and Roger, confined within a yellowing wicker basket, was bundled inside. They left with the driver looking decidedly shaky and leaning from his side window.

Later that evening they returned empty-handed with the news that Roger had been kept under strict observation prior to possible minor surgery. Maybe, they had been told, they could collect him in forty-eight hours. Life was sweeter in Loftus Road that Monday night. There was also general rejoicing on the Tuesday. However, by 5 o'clock on the following day all were aware of Roger's return.

'Well,' I said brightly as I met the girls in the hallway, 'and how's the patient, eh?'

Ange looked at me moist-eyed and blew hard into a pink tissue. 'Oh Mr Hebingdon', she gulped, 'you will never guess what they done to him. Never! They, they –' she stopped and looked to Eff for support. 'Go on,' rapped Eff addressing the ceiling, 'don't bugger about – tell 'im! Tell 'im what the swine done! Go on – tell 'im!'

Ange suppressed a sob. 'Alright', she said, 'Ay will. Yes. Yes, Ay will. They, they – cut-his-tail-off-Mr Hebingdon, that's what they done – cut-off-his-tail!'

'What *all* of it?' I said, aghast.

'*All* of it,' said Eff. 'Right up. Gotta ninch left he 'as. With a dolly on it.'

'But why?' I asked, 'I mean . . .'

Ange's eyes refilled. 'Ay do not know Mr Hebingdon, reely Ay don't. Perhaps they thought if he 'ad not got no tail to stick hup, he would stop sticking it.' The floodgates opened again. 'Excuse me,' she said, 'Ay must go to the toilet.' Clearly she was under a strain.

Eff glared at me. 'Told you he was a ponce, didn't I?' she said. And turned on her heel.

Unbelievably the shock therapy worked. Ponce though he may have been in the jaundiced eyes of Eff, Roger's doctor did the trick. I have yet to receive a satisfactory medical explanation as to why the metamorphosis occurred, but Roger's elevation from common mog to ersatz Manx certainly made life more bearable in Loftus Road. But I was still not enamoured of the street. Nor of the district.

Shepherd's Bush, which lies like a seedy and disowned relation between prodigious Holland Park and less sought-after Acton, is bisected by the Uxbridge Road. This is layered with old newspapers, discarded soft drinks and beer cans and other jetsam of a consumer society, and flanked by liquor marts, betting shops and Eastern take-aways. It is also remarkable for a grease-patinaed eating house named Jack Horner's House of Pies, the products of which contributed in no small way to the ambience of the thoroughfare, and an Asian-supervised establishment advertising itself as 'specialists in Oriental and Greek delicacies and wine'. The claim, as I discovered, was pure braggadocio.

Eager for a sensual reminder of the Cyclades I visited it but once. 'Good morning,' I said, my palate sharpening in anticipation as I crossed the threshold, 'a bottle of Domestica please.' The proprietor gazed at me sadly from behind a wall of poppadoms and wagged his head from side to side like an agitated metronome. 'So sorry sir,' he said, 'not stocking cleaning fluids. Try hardware person over road. Very good fellow, isn't it?'

Loftus Road sported no such emporia. It was strictly residential. Running at right-angles from the main artery of Shepherd's Bush and lined with plane trees much patronised by dogs, delinquents and passing itinerant foreign nationals in physical distress, it had a bakery at one end and the Queen's Park Rangers football ground at the other. Between the two extremes were at least two houses of ill repute. Daily these discharged their clientele between the hours of two and four in the morning; and to judge from the sound of breaking glass and West Indian voices raucously demanding their money back or some other form of compensation, they appeared to be substandard. The small hours were seldom silent in Loftus Road. Nor were they muted in other streets within the zone.

Aptly named Commonwealth Avenue and Tunis Road, South Africa and Bloemfontein, to example but a few, they housed a representative selection from every part of the globe upon which Victoria's sun once steadfastly refused to set. All lived together in contented racial disharmony.

On Mondays, Wednesdays and Fridays forays were made by the intellectually impoverished natives upon the Pakistanis and Indians; on Thursdays and Fridays the West Indians played the English; and on Saturdays the Irish had a go at whoever they saw first when the pubs had emptied. Quite properly, Sunday was observed as a rest day by all but the very ungodly and, excluding the Asian community, reserved for getting drunk. Tedious though life may have been in Shepherd's Bush, it was never dull. But it was on football match days that the pulse of the neighbourhood really quickened.

Until I lived in Loftus Road, I knew little about Association Football. The name Queen's Park Rangers meant nothing to me. Nor did those of other participants of the game. However, after only one experience of making my way up Loftus Road against a tide of disgruntled football supporters coming from the opposite direction in an aura of mixed ales and hate, the instinct for self-preservation prompted me to learn by heart the dates and times of every home fixture for the season, including those scheduled to be played in the evenings, and the origins and behavioural patterns of the visiting teams. Having established these I arranged either to be in another part of the metropolis or to put myself under house arrest during the hours immediately preceding and following the playing periods. Nevertheless, irksome though those spells of self-imposed imprisonment could be, they were both educative and entertaining. Particularly my evening confinements. I witnessed some macabre spectacles through my unwashed window panes.

The stadium was hidden from Loftus Road, but my bedroom window looked diagonally toward it and at the floodlighting installations standing around the ground. They reached skywards like giant flyswats ready to strike. Three hours before an evening kick-off they would be switched on, drenching my room with sodium lighting, unreal and cold and turning the night to day. And in the street below, exposed in the blue-white light, the hamburger and hotdog vendors would set up their stalls, beating their arms across their chests to arrest the winter cold and drizzle, while an ageing, white-stubbled rosette seller displaying his favours on a totem pole took station opposite. From around the corner would come the noise of the horse boxes of the police being parked and discharging their mounts and then the clip-clop of hooves and the jingle of saddlery as they came into view to stand in pairs, flank to flank, on opposite sides of the street.

Then, first in ones and quiet twos and then in trios and quartets and later in gaggles and in noisy hunting packs, the funny-hatted fans would arrive and tramp their way toward the gates, hands thrust deep into the pockets of

78

unbuttoned, flapping weather-proofs and trailing long woollen scarves thrice wound around their necks. Some walked with their eyes fixedly set upon the ground, some scuffed and loped their ways, upending beer cans as they went and jettisoning the empties, others with heads held high and staring insolently from right to left with mouths agape – eager for trouble and anxious to prove the machismo – swaggered past and made two-fingered gestures to the unheeding police; but all passed by my window in an hour-long stream.

A straggle of panting late-comers, shouting over their shoulders to tardier companions would run below me, and with their disappearance a temporary peace would come to Loftus Road. The hotdog salesmen would refresh themselves with their own wares, the rosette hawker would scratch himself, shoulder his denuded totem pole and limp away, the police horses would move to around the corner; and from a basement opposite, a bent, grey-haired old lady in curlers would appear with a bucket and shovel and scrape up the still warm evidence of their previous occupation. She never missed a match and presented herself with clockwork regularity both then and after the crowd's departure at the end of the game. So too, did Eff and Ange; but not for material gain. Their presence was motivated by prurient curiosity.

To Eff and Ange the unrehearsed dramas which accompanied the final rites and exodus from a football match at Loftus Road made compulsive viewing and were attractions bettered only by street accidents or embroidered accounts of other women's operations. Accordingly, and within minutes of the last airborne boos, jeers and counter cheers coming from the ground, they would arrive in my room for a bird's-eye view of the hoped for mayhem to come. They were seldom disappointed.

A home win ensured that the wearers of blue and white scarves tunelessly and adenoidally advised their beaten opponents that they were the champions and furthermore, they they would never walk alone, to which the vanquished would respond with a full-throated chorus of blasphemy and obscenities, and then run nail files along the sides of any unattended parked vehicles. If the home side was defeated the roles were reversed. However, regardless of the outcome and in the best sporting traditions of contemporary English soccer meetings, a vociferous minority of rival supporters would hack, punch, kick and slash each other until separated by a long-suffering police force and bundled into black marias.

Also included in the cast of thousands were those who were too drunk to remember which side they had come to support. Caring friends, often enjoying a similar state of painlessness, would lead them uncertainly from the main scene of action and place them carefully on the nearby low stone walls which fronted the basement houses. And there they would sit, staring to their front in an unseeing alcoholic haze, wearing pom-pommed caps and idiot smiles, and sublimely indifferent to the carnage before them. From time to time, like drunken Humpty Dumpties and still in a sitting position, some would slowly topple backward and out of sight to the basement below, only to be hauled into view once more by equally slow-moving companions and reassuringly patted into place again. On the last occasion the girls and I occupied ringside seats one such inebriate gave no less than three encores, celebrating his final curtain call by impartially being sick over both of his assistants. Like a former Queen of England, they were not amused. Nor were Eff and Ange. But they were gratified.

'H'm!' snapped Eff, elbowing Ange out of the way to get a better view of the cameo, 'that'll take some getting off that will! Tch! tch! tch!' Her dentures chattered with satisfaction. 'Look at 'em – just look at 'em! Filth, that's what they are – filth!'

'Yes,' agreed Ange, re-establishing her position with difficulty and grasping the curtain, 'they are. They are haminals Mr Hebingdon, nothing but haminals! Still', she reflected and pausing to savour a past horror, 'they are not as bad as the Manchester lot. No! No, the Manchestrians are reely haminal. Yes. Yes, Ay would not demean myself by telling you what they done, er did, when they come 'ere, here.'

'Really?' I said, one eye on the unhappy trio below, who by now had been detribalised by their immediate neighbours and were engaged in isolated and slow-motion fisticuffs. 'Well they must have been pretty frightful.'

'They was,' emphasised Ange, raising her voice to top the sound of a breaking window further down the road, 'they *was*! They . . .'

She paused again and drew in her breath sharply as dreadful memories flooded back. 'They blew up', she said, and speaking in capitals, 'certain things.'

I looked toward her, puzzled. 'Certain, things?' I asked.

'Yes Mr Hebingdon,' she repeated, narrowing her eyes in the sodium lighting and continuing to italicise, 'certain things. Dozens of them. And then they let them –'

'Dozens?' said Eff, disparagingly, ''undreds more like

it; and all colours an' all – blues, greens, reds, pinks –'

'What – balloons?' I said, anxious not to believe the worst of the northern tribes and also a little misled by the ambiguous reference to the multiplicity of the rainbow, 'do you mean they –'

'No! No! No! No! No!' said Eff impatiently, 'you know – whatsits.'

Ange took a deep breath. 'Quantrums,' she said. 'They blew up quantrums.'

I never did witness the mass inflation and liberation of that particular Mancunian mascot, although I was still in residence when the team came south again. But the thought of Ange's quantrum theory continues to disturb me at inappropriate moments. And even though many years have passed since I last breathed the Roger-laden air of Shepherd's Bush, I often think of her; and with affection. Unlike her overweight and ungenerous companion, Ange was a good person who did me many kindnesses and in a strange way I became very fond of her.

She brought me hot whiskey and milk when I was unwell, put folded newspaper under my mattress to mute the squeaking of its springs and chased the dust from one side of the room to the other. And in the summer she would invite me to sit in the overgrown, cat-smelling patch which served as a garden and tell me of the days when the neighbourhood prospered and was respectable, and even a chemist lived in Loftus Road. And she would look up at the roof with its missing slates, and sigh.

She became very quiet the day I told her I had bought a flat in Kenton and would be leaving. 'Yes,' she said thoughtfully, 'Ay thought you would. Only the other day Ay said to Eff, Ay said Ay think Mr Hebingdon will be moving soon, Ay said. And Eff said what, because of the ballcock? And Ay said no, it is nothing to do with the ballcock Ay said, it is just not his cup of tea 'ere, here, Ay said. And Eff said. . . .' She paused. 'Well Ay will not tell you what Eff responded Mr Hebingdon because it was common, but . . .' She paused again and glanced furtively over her left shoulder as if sensing her companion's presence. 'She do not like you Mr Hebingdon. Not since them words you 'ad, er, had about her hopening your letters by mistake. You remember, Mr Hebingdon? You recall that little, ahem! mistake?'

'Yes,' I said, the steam marks on the flap of the envelope still fresh in my memory, 'I do.' 'But anyway,' said Ange returning to the present, 'Ay was right, was I not? Still,' she continued, 'it is a nice place, Kenton is.' 'You know it?' I asked. Ange nodded. 'Slaightly. Ay once kept company with a man from Kenton', she said wistfully, 'but he cut his throat. In the toilet. Fred his name was.' Momentarily her eyes misted, and then brightened. 'Ay expect you will have your own there? A toilet, I mean?' 'Oh yes,' I said, 'I think so . . .'

She cried when I left and kissed me abrasively on both cheeks; and she waved a sodden handkerchief to me from the open mauve front door as I drove away. Eff was conspicuous by her absence. Nor was I able to bid farewell to Orca. He was in the bath.

4

Kenton – not Wembley

I was relieved when I moved from Shepherd's Bush to Kenton. So was my elderly mother who lived in darkest Farnham, in Surrey. Close to Northwick park and Harrow-on-the-Hill with its school and parish church of St Mary's, the venue had a better ring to it and smacked of respectability. Comfortable with early memories, my mother associated the district with Betjeman verse and broad-brimmed boaters, to say nothing of Byron and Churchill. She was less happy when I advised her that my postal address would be Wembley. Wembley, she considered, sounded common and refused to include the name when addressing letters to me. Consequently, not only did she succeed in causing friction between myself and the local postal authorities who plainly regarded the omission as a slight to the locale, but she ensured that all her correspondence took a minimum of three weeks to reach my flat before dropping on to the mat heavily scored and with the name Kenton savagely crossed out in red crayon. On one unfortunate occasion and having taxed the patience of the sorting office for some while, she posted a parcel to me. Too large to be forced through the letter box, it was delivered to me in person by an aggrieved and aggressive employee.

Kenton – not Wembley

'*Wembley*,' he said, stabbing the package with a muscular and none too clean finger, 'that's where you live mate. Wembley – not bloody Kenton.' He glared at me. 'Got anything against Wembley mate?' 'No,' I said meekly, 'nothing at all. Actually it's my mother.' 'Oh *is* it,' he said, continuing to eye me with disfavour, 'well tell 'er then.' He thrust the packet into my hand and started down the stairs, pausing only to confide in a rubber plant on the landing. 'Toffee-nosed bastard,' he muttered, and went out of my life confirming Bernard Shaw's judgement that it is impossible for an Englishman to open his mouth without making some other Englishman despise him.

He left me thinking wistfully of another period in my life when I lived in a village where the postman safely delivered all the mail by hand, appraised the recipient of its source of origin and not infrequently gave a précis of the contents. He was a nice man and the whole community mourned when he was detained during Her Majesty's pleasure – not for interfering with the post, but with small boys. Little remained private in that leafy backwater of south-east England. Nor, as I was to discover, did it in the cherry-treed environs of Kenton.

The flat into which I moved was one in a small purpose-built block of six. Accurately, it was described by the estate agent who left the district shortly after the sale to breed chickens on the Isle of Wight as, 'in immaculate condition, possessed of full central heating, a fully-tiled bathroom and was', in his opinion, 'easy to run'. He was correct in every particular. What he neglected to include in the list of superlatives was that the premises were endowed with the finest intelligence network in the North London area. Its agents worked silently and in the highest traditions of the service; and had it not been for a minor lack of attention to detail by one of their women operatives, I would have remained ignorant of the force's presence.

The mental aberration occurred a week before I took up residence and during one of my daily excursions to my new home. Carrying a reconditioned vacuum cleaner, unashamedly bearing a label advertising its return to the working world in block capitals, and festooned with carrier bags each marked with the name of a London store, I made my way past the downstairs flat *en route* to my own on the floor above. As I did so the door opened revealing a cigarette-smoking lady accoutred in a quilted housecoat and clasping an empty milk bottle.

Her eyes fastened first upon the legend attached to the hoover, narrowed swiftly as she digested the message, constricted still further as they flitted to a bag emblazoned Co-Op, and finally came to rest on me. A length of ash dropped from her cigarette. 'Morning,' she said, 'lovely day.' And retreating backwards, still holding the empty bottle, slowly she closed the door upon me. It was a minor slip in the game of domestic espionage but enough to tell me that my social and financial status had been logged.

I mentioned the incident to the gentleman who was doing my interior decorating. He evinced no surprise. 'Oh 'er,' he said, and gave a throaty chuckle. 'Been up and down the stairs like a yo-yo all week she 'as, peeking through the door. Oh yes. Felt the wallpaper an' all. "'Essian?" she said, "'essian? That set 'im back a bit," she said.' He chuckled again and stroked his paintbrush against the rim of the tin. 'Still,' he advanced, 'she's 'armless guv. Just bleedin' bored and nosey. They all are –

. . . accoutred in a quilted housecoat . . .

the women that is. Know wadamin guv?' I nodded.

'Oh yes,' he said, and repeated his appraisal. 'They know what you paid for the place, they've got the name of the 'fridge – bit surprised you're going to cook with the electrics an' that, but what's really worrying them', he continued, 'is why you 'aven't moved in yet. Like old Nosey Parker said yesterday, it's six weeks since 'e exchanged contracts she said, and I know 'e wanted the sale through sharpish.'

He paused to work the finishing top coat into the door lintel and feathered it. 'Anyway,' he concluded, standing back to admire his handiwork, 'there's no 'arm in them. Not reely. At least they're not into wife-swapping – not like they are in 'Arrer. On-the-'ill that is.' He paused again and closed on me. 'You'd be amazed', he confided into my left ear, 'at what goes on in 'Arrer-on-the-'ill.' And nudged me. 'Yes,' I said, 'I'm sure I would.' So too, I thought, would my mother.

I spent some time pondering on that morning's events. Intrigued though I was by the unsolicited character assassination of the good burghers of Harrow and the alleged dolce vita which took place on the Hill, I was more impressed with the speed and accuracy with which my own dossier had been compiled. Also, having made a brief acquaintance with one member of the network, I wondered what manner of people lived behind the other closed doors in the block. I had to curb my impatience. Although I heard them, several weeks were to elapse before I glimpsed them; and several more before we exchanged courtesies. Suburban flat dwellers, I was soon to learn, were wary of strangers; and particularly strangers with hessian wallpaper.

88

Kenton – not Wembley

They were a strangely assorted company in the flats. The top floor respectively housed an unmarried lapsed lady Salvationist of uncertain years, and a bachelor Doctor of Philosophy of uncertain habits. He earned his living by lecturing on the mysteries of electrical engineering at a London polytechnic, and my undying hatred for his indifferent playing of 'Jesus Joy of Man's Desiring' on an out-of-tune upright piano every third Sunday. Also included in his many idiosyncrasies was an uncontrollable diurnal impulse to re-arrange his furniture, stick by stick, between the hours of midnight and 2am across the uncarpeted floor above me.

The flat opposite to mine was occupied by a young Japanese couple with jet black hair, painted smiles and lacquered manners. She worked behind a grille in an oriental bank and he exercised his skills in the kitchens of an oriental restaurant. To judge from the contents of their plastic dustbin which stood with others in a ground floor common storeroom, they appeared to live on an exclusive diet of raw fish and All Bran. This could have accounted for their physical appearance. Even by Japanese standards they were very spare. By contrast, the occupant of the flat below them was a very large and unremarkable member of the Metropolitan Police Force.

Lastly, but by no means least, the home beneath me was that of the inefficient lady member of MI5 who had blown her cover. She lived with an ageing black poodle with homosexual tendencies and a passion for the stand-pipe in the communal gardens, and a middle-aged husband who had what appeared to be a standing order for hernia repairs with the local hospital. He also had psoriasis and a hollow tooth, and I suspected his favourite reading matter

89

` was *Gray's Anatomy*. One soon learned not to ask him how he was. Once, before I knew better, I did so. He folded his hands carefully over his much surgically explored region and jerked his head in the direction of Northwick Park Hospital. 'They want to have another look inside,' he husked, 'week after next.' And sucked his tooth. 'That'll be the fourth', he said, 'this year.' I made sympathetic noises. 'Still', I said, looking at his hands, 'the psoriasis seems to be better.' Reluctantly he agreed. 'Yes,' he said, 'I suppose it is; but me dandruff's playing 'avoc with me collar.'

We were strange bedfellows, but saving the latterday Mata Hari, we had one thing in common. We all commuted by road or rail to London Town. And so did most of Kenton. It was a pattern of life, constant and unvaried and in which all shared for five days of the week.

Daily, alarm clocks – the cockerels of suburbia – opened unwilling sleep-encrusted eyes, and in a thousand flats and semis and detacheds pyjama-clad encumbents yawned, rose to look through double glazing at their lawns, and at red-painted plastic gnomes with fishing rods and funny hats, staring unseeingly into plastic pools. An armpit scratch or two, another yawn, thence to the kitchen to switch on the radio and electric kettle, and so to the bathroom to perform the opening rites for yet another day, while Radios 1 or 2 – or even 4 and 3 – blared or murmured as the razors buzzed. Then on a wave of aftershave and fully dressed in office suiting, off the peg from Austin Reed, it was back to the kitchenette for instant coffee or instant tea, a bowl of cereal or a slice of toast, and instant indigestion.

For some, there was an absent-minded goodbye peck

and a 'bye-bye-dear-and-have-a-good-day' as children
were force-fed and jacketed for school; for singletons, just
silence as transistors clicked to sleep and gamexes were
donned in halls; and by 8 o'clock a thousand Halcyons and
Avalons had closed their doors. And as blackbirds sang to
the clitter and clatter and deep tumty-tum hum from
nearby railway tracks, so the worker bees of Kenton left
their hives in search of nectar for their queens, and the
well-tried trek to the station began.

Off they went in ones and twos, drawn from avenues
named Grassmere, Derwent, Coniston and Thirlmere –
Lakeland by-ways of suburbia, housing Wordsworths and
Patels – past snowcemed pebble-dashed square houses with
neater tiny squares of lawns edged with statutory
aubretias, past doorways with black cats *in situ*, slit-eyed
and pensive in the sun, sitting next to empty bottles
washed and ready for collection by Unigate and other
dairies, under lilacs, limes, laburnums, over a bridge
daubed with graffiti – 'TV time for Communists' – all on
their way to Northwick Park.

Silently they bought their *Guardians*, *Telegraphs* and
Mails and *Suns* from the kiosk in the subway, waved
season tickets at the barrier, all ignoring the collector –
Jamaican, spectacled and comely, with a badge saying
'Jesus Loves Me' – and mutely waited for the metro, to
arrive on Platform One.

Then, as the stopping train from Watford spilled out
students for the Harrow Tech – bomber-jacketed and
frayed-jeaned and eating Mars bars on the move, they
jostled through its impatient guard-regulated doors to sit
or strap-hang to their journeys end and to be crushed still
more at Preston Road and Wembley Park, each wrapped

in a cloak of anonymity and nose-deep in crosswords, sports reports, or Page Three of the *Sun*. And at the close of a working day, city-soiled and tired, they would stand three-tiered at Baker Street, all reading *Evening Standard*s. Twenty minutes later out they would pour, mostly unfulfilled, but happier than when they had left at 8.15am. Some might even say 'goodnight' to smiling, black fat 'Jesus Loves Me' or Irish Mick the atheist, but most would merely grunt and elbow past them, as aphasic as in the morning.

Down the stairs they would go and out into the street to waiting cars and buses; to padlocked cycles chained to railings; to waiting wives with waiting dogs, and Home-sweet, mortgaged Home. Back! Back in time for the Archers and a Gin and T, a meal of convenience food, and then TV; and so to bed in a G-planned room, to sleep and dream perchance of summer holidays in Greece, until the alarm bell rang again.

It was some while before I realised that I was one of their number.

There was however, another category of passengers who patronised the Metropolitan Line. Those were they who travelled from 10 o'clock onward when the cheap day fares came into operation. As often as not the bulk of them were either elderly or in their late 'teens, or pregnant. The first section were usually equipped with National Health spectacles and dentures to match, while the representatives of England's youth were invariably decorated with a safety-pin through one ear and headphones around both. They gazed vacantly ahead of them with glazed expressions and their feet on the opposite seat. If denied the benefit of personal Walkman

92

stereos, they adopted similar postures, chewed their finger nails and eyed their seniors with cultivated insolence. I would not have invited them to tea. Conversely, the ladies who carried the future generation within them without additional travelling costs, had little time to be bored. Nor were they allowed the luxury of private thought or silent prayer. Frequently attended by blessings of earlier unions who forced them into non-stop conversation to which the whole compartment became privy, their lives were laid bare and often my heart bled for them. But no young mother-to-be was more deserving of universal sympathy than the one whose martyrdom I witnessed one Monday morning.

Moon-faced and floral-smocked and heavy with her unborn load and accompanied by a four-year-old boy-child clutching a half-chewed apple, she staggered through the train doors at Preston Road and collapsed into the seat opposite to me. 'Strewth!' she gasped, and popped a Polo into her mouth.

Next to her, her first-born stretched out its free hand toward the packet and started to grizzle. It was an unpleasing child with a runny nose and, as time disclosed, an equally unstaunchable curiosity. 'Want one,' it demanded, and flung the apple into her lap.

'Ou!' she said, as it bounced off her unseen son or daughter, 'stoppit Wayne, stoppit at once! Could have made poor Mummy choke that could! Now be quiet, don't fidget and', she added, returning the jading fruit to its owner, 'echerapple before it goes brown.' Her horrid heir looked at his Golden Delicious with growing disenchantment and shook his head. 'Wanter Polo,' he repeated.

93

His mother gave a suck of exasperation. 'No you don't,' she contradicted, 'Wayne does *not* want a Polo. Wayne's got his nice apple. It's Mummy that needs Polos because of the baby – it's baby that makes Mummy want Polos. Wayne isn't having a baby, is he?' she enquired rhetorically. Reluctantly Wayne agreed. 'Well all right then,' said his mother, 'now shut up.'

Across the aisle a sixty-year-old eaves-dropper with a blue rinse and tinted glasses nodded understandingly. 'Carrots,' she confided to her friend in the adjoining seat, 'that's what it was with me. Carrots. Couldn't go an hour without me carrots I couldn't. Not an hour. Funny isn't it?' 'Um,' said her friend, 'yes it is, yes. With me it was sardines. In oil.' Opposite to me the glucose-craver mechanically addressed herself to another offering, looked at the window, and sucked. It was, I thought, a mercy that she had not become addicted to sardines. With or without oil. Also, I conjectured vaguely as to where she was going; and why.

It was not long before I was enlightened. Apple-weary, bored and catarrhal and having explored first his nose and then his less accessible parts, Wayne returned to his mother. 'Mum-may,' he shrilled adenoidally and loudly, 'Why are you going to the hospital Mum-may?' Across the way Blue Rinse pricked up her ears.

'Check up,' said Mummay continuing to look out of the window and suck, 'that's why Mummy's going to the hospital – for a check up.' Blue Rinse nudged her neighbour. 'To see about the bay-bay Mum-may?' pursued Wayne. 'That's right,' said Mummay addressing the passing landscape and increasing her rate of salivation, 'to see about the baby, to see if baby's alright.'

94

'I hope it is.'

'Yes, so does Mummy dear.'

'Yes. Mum-may?'

'Um?'

'Mum-may, will the bay-bay come today Mum-may?'

'No dear, not today,' said Mummay communicating directly with her offspring and acknowledging the blatant interest of Blue Rinse and her companion together with that of a weedy man with a hairpiece and impaired hearing who had lowered his paper and joined the Wayne fan club, 'baby won't come today and wipe your nose.'

'But why won't bay-bay come today Mum-may?'

'Because it won't, it doesn't want to, it's not ready and don't sniff it's common.'

'But suppose it does Mum-ma –'

'It *won't*. And-what-have-you-done-with-it-I-gave-you-a-clean-one-before-we-left. Honestly I –'

'But if it does Mum-may, supposing bay-bay came in the train Mum-may, would you have to pay for it?'

'No dear no, Mummy wouldn't have to pay for it – here's a tissue, use that, reely the questions they ask, he never stops you know – it's the same with the telly – who's that man, where's his mummy, what did he have for breakfast – on and on and on and you have to answer them don't you, they won't take no will they?' 'No,' said Blue Rinse, 'they won't, no.' 'What?' said Hairpiece, leaning forward and cupping his hand. 'She said they won't take no,' said Blue Rinse, raising her voice. Hairpiece looked puzzled. 'Who won't?' he asked. 'Kiddies,' bellowed Blue Rinse, 'kiddies won't –'

'Mum-may?'

'Oh Gawd! Yes dear?'

'Suppose,' said Wayne playing his trump card, 'suppose it came when you were on the toilet?'

Unfortunately for posterity I was unable to record Mum-may's reply. Wayne's ace was presented as we pulled into Baker Street, but as I left the compartment I could not help thinking that there was every chance of him ceasing to be an only child before his mother reached Aldgate.

That I was enabled to abandon the early morning commuter rush and privileged to join the post 10 o'clock elite was due entirely to the expertise of two distinguished surgeons. Together, and in return for substantial fees they arranged that I should be rendered unconscious within the Clementine Churchill Hospital in Harrow-on-the-Hill, wheeled into its operating theatre and then placed in a foetal position upon a table. That accomplished they flexed their muscles, attacked my lumbar spine and did dreadful things to it with instruments both blunt and sharp. When their work was over, and after a decent interval, they sat beside my bed like Tweedledum and Tweedledee, and beamed at me. It was New Year's Eve.

'Mr Ebdon,' said one, a South African with an enviable reputation and a built-in sniff, 'all is very well. In twilve months tarm you will be as rart as ren.' 'As right as rain,' endorsed his colleague smoothly, and patted my arm. 'Gentlemen,' I said, returning their courtesy and ringing my bell for some more pain killers, 'I'm glad to hear it. Thank you both.' 'Not at all,' they said, 'it was a pleasure.' And advising me that upon my release I should take two months off, sit as little as possible, avoid mechanised travel and walk everywhere, they wished me a Happy New Year and left, leaving me staring at the ceiling and wondering how I should take to life as a horse.

Their advice was sound and I followed it in every particular. I learned how to write lying down and to eat standing up; I walked everywhere within a radius of 10 miles and became proud of my calves and ashamed of my shoes. However, tedious though it was, my new mode of living did have compensations. It allowed me to see another side of Kenton, an aspect hitherto denied me and which revealed itself each morning when the commuter torrent to the station had trickled to a stream and then dried up.

As the curtain of a play falls upon one act and rises on another, so it did on the Kenton stage. The scene changed and new characters appeared in many guises: housewives, milkmen, traders, children and those of three score years and five. Some, track-suited and wearing knitted hats with pom-poms on them and risking cardiac fatigue, puffed and wheezed their ways around the playing fields of Northwick Park, steaming as they jogged. Others, more circumspectly, exercised their dogs, unleashing them to chase the gulls which winter always brings to the ill-drained turf, or commanded them to 'Sit!' or 'Stay!' Most did neither and were told they were naughty or downright bad, but they cared not a jot and jumped up and down, then ran away leering with pink lolling tongues to violate the nearest bush. And their owners threw their hands in the air and gathered in conclave in midfield and vowed they would never bring them again. But they did, and each day I watched the pantomime repeated by Pekes and Poms and Kerry Blues and those of uncertain pedigree.

I saw dogs being patted and dogs being smacked,

friendly dogs with wagging tails, satanic dogs who bit each other and idiot dogs who bit their keepers, and daily, promptly at half past nine, a cantering brindle Dane would appear, dragging its owner behind it. Small, podgy and panting, she flew across the field with streaming hair and reddening face and shouting to the beast to stop, but it never did and scarcely a day passed without the poor woman completing the course on her stomach. It was fine entertainment and a useful time check, for she was as punctual as a Greenwich Time Pip. But there were other creatures of habit too: the pram and basket pushers of Kenton.

The perambulators, usually transporting nothing more dangerous than a baby or two and a soiled pink woolly elephant, were innocuous; so were the mothers who wheeled them. The baskets however, were a different proposition. Fashioned from wicker and mounted on wheels from which sharp axle-heads protruded and upon which Boadicea would have looked with envy, they could, and did, prove devastating. Favoured by elderly and myopic ladies often capable of moving at speeds which belied their age, daily they were trundled erratically from quiet backwaters toward the shopping centre and I grew to fear them. Particularly on Fridays; for it was then they mounted their major offensive.

As bees assembling prior to swarming, they appeared on the horizon in ones and twos, grew in numbers as they neared the Kenton Road, and massed at the pelican crossing. There, wheel to wheel and axle to axle, they waited for the bleeps and then, with heads down and thoughts a thousand miles away, they charged across the road like rampant Iceni, scything the shins of oncoming

98

pedestrians as they went, and through the supermarket doors. Once inside they parked their infernal machines in untidy rows, equipped themselves with wire trolleys, no less lethal, urgently dispersed and careered shortsightedly among the other shoppers, their progress marked by the clatter of falling tins and the yelps and oaths of their unintended victims. Blissfully unaware of their created carnage and mayhem they pressed on, filled their trolleys with cut-price toilet tissues, tasty chicken cat food and special offer Rich Tea biscuits, propelled them with undiminished speed toward the cash points where, having completed the circuit in record time, they arrested the flow of customers for ten minutes and more while they searched for their purses. That mission accomplished, they delayed further transactions with other vendors for another five minutes while completing their own, transferred their purchases into their personal chariots, and leaving bedlam behind them, gathered in knots outside the store to have a chat and adjust their wigs.

They were a formidable section of Kenton society and tempered by experience I learned to avoid them; but not before I had become an early casualty of one of them. Queen of the Charioteers and unquestionably a descendant of Ben Hur, she was a wiry little woman in her late sixties wearing a close-fitting pink hat made of nylon petals, and a pair of thick lensed spectacles. Attempting, but failing by inches to cut across my bows, she caught me a glancing blow on my left ankle, drawing blood from the graze and a stream of invective from me.

'Oo-er!' she exclaimed, startled by my vehemence. 'Well really I –'

'I'm very sorry,' I said, rolling down my sock to inspect

the damage, 'I –'

'I should think so too,' she snapped, 'you ought to go and wash your mouth out young man, that's what you ought to do – with soap! You –' she stopped abruptly as her handiwork swam into focus. 'Did I do *that*?' she asked, her eyes widening in disbelief and dismay. 'Did I really do *that*?'

'Please,' I said, balancing on one leg and supporting myself against the window of a delicatessen and coffee shop trading under the name of Goodies, 'it's nothing really, I –'

'But it *is*,' she insisted, hypnotised by the wound. 'Oh dear! Oh dear! Oh dear! Oh dear! I am sorry, really I am! Here – spit on this and dab it.' And overcome with remorse she handed me a tissue.

'Tsk! tsk! tsk!' she said as she watched it discolour, 'Know what I think dear? I think we should both go and have a nice sit down, don't you? A nice sit down and a cuppa? My hubby used to say there's nothing like a nice sit down and a cuppa when you're upset. And I *am* dear,' she continued, fanning herself with the local newspaper, 'I really am. Quite queasy really – know what I mean?' I nodded understandingly. 'What a good idea,' I said, by now feeling responsible for her state of shock, 'I'd love to.' And together we tottered into Goodies.

She was a neat, chatty little London sparrow of a woman smelling faintly of stale lily-of-the-valley and fresh gin, and as the throb in my ankle lessened I warmed to her over our coffee. Off the streets and divorced from her basket she was, I discovered, quite harmless.

'Always pop in here on Fridays,' she said, heaping brown sugar into her cup and stirring it vigorously, 'pensions Thursdays, big shopping Fridays; and then Goodies.' Still stirring she looked around her approvingly. 'Nice place really,' she said. 'Kosher of course – all "oh my life" and what have you but their bread's lovely. And anyway,' she added, 'they can't help being Jews can they?' She took a sip of her coffee holding the cup in both hands, her elbows on the table. 'Been in Kenton long dear?'

I shook my head. 'No,' I said, 'about eighteen months.' Behind the glasses sharp eyes looked at me inquisitively. 'Like it?' she asked. 'Well,' I said, 'I haven't had time to explore it properly yet'; and explained my position. She tut-tutted sympathetically and pulled a face. 'Nasty,' she said, 'nasty things, operations', and gave me a long and detailed account of her daughter's hysterectomy. 'But you'll like Kenton dear,' she said, returning to the original topic and topping up her now lukewarm coffee, 'when you get to know it, that is. Lovely place it is. Friendly. People say good morning and that. Know what I mean?'

Elbows still in place, she sipped noisily from the freshly filled cup and smiled nostalgically across its rim, and past me. 'I'll never forget the first time we saw it – my hubby and me that is. Just after the war it was, in the autumn. We'd come from Camden Town, and we came out of the station on the hill up there and looked down this road – it was all sunlit I remember, and Stan said to me, he said "Doris," he said, "could be the seaside couldn't it?" And I know what he meant: because there were your houses on both sides and your actual sky above them; and the sea could have been there, out of sight, just beyond the buildings. And I thought it was lovely. So did Stan.

101

He's gone now of course. Cancer. Last Christmas . . .'

Suddenly she was silent, mechanically sipping, and decades away in memory. Then, just as suddenly, she returned to the present. 'Mind you,' she said, spooning the sugar from the bottom of her cup and looking across the street at two sari-clad women and a deeply tanned Caribbean gentleman who were passing the China Diner Take-Away, 'things have changed and I won't pretend I like it, because I don't. I mean forty years ago there wasn't none of them about, but now . . .'

She nodded toward the Asians and shook her head in silent disapproval. '*And* we've got Chinks,' she said. 'Not that I'm racial,' she added hastily, 'I mean God made them all, didn't he? Black, brown, yellow – the lot. I mean, they've as much right to live as we have, haven't they? Yes. And I'm sure they're quite nice, some of them. All the same,' she concluded, replacing her cup on its saucer and ferreting in her handbag, 'the house prices don't half drop when they move in next door to you. Know what I mean?'

She dabbed primly at the corners of her mouth with a tissue, screwed it up and dropped it into the empty cup. 'Well dear,' she said, 'I've enjoyed our little chat'. 'So have I,' I said, and reached for the bill. Arthritic fingers rapped the back of my hand. 'Ah! Ah!' she said, 'my treat.'

It was the first of several meetings between us, but thankfully the only one on which she drew blood. She was a forceful little character with a strident voice and trenchant views which she was not afraid to express in public. She also possessed an invaluable knowledge of local shops and their keepers and I became indebted to her.

'Wouldn't go in there dear,' she shrilled as I made to enter the local butchers on the second occasion we met, 'doesn't know his rump from his brisket he doesn't. *And* he's common.' Plainly within earshot the subject of her disapprobation glowered at her through the open door and took it out on a leg of pork with a cleaver. 'Ken Foster's', she continued imperatively and regardless of the laws of slander, 'that's where you ought to go dear – up on the Hill. Lovely man he is. So's his mince – all pink and fresh it is. Know what I mean? And if he's not there, ask for Roy; and tell him I sent you – they all know me up there.' I did not doubt her. Indeed after only two meetings I had formed the opinion that most people would know of her; and not only in Kenton and Harrow-on-the-Hill. But her appreciation of Mr Foster was sound. As I was to find out, he was a lovely man.

He was a Happy Families butcher. His girth was wide and so was his smile and he had a soft pink face, soft pink hands and moved in an aura of lard and sawdust. So too did Roy and Keith and Harold, his assistants; and they all reacted to my sponsor's name.

'Ah! Mrs H,' said Mr Foster, beaming and wiping his hands on his apron and offering me the right one, 'very fond of her mince Mrs H is.' 'Not 'arf,' endorsed Roy doing likewise, 'she likes her mince, Mrs H does.' 'Um,' said Keith, 'but it gets behind her plate she says.' And they all fell about and waved knives in the air, and asked me what they could do for me.

They were a jolly quartet who won my custom and respect, for here were men with expertise, who cared for their customers' requirements. Glowingly they would expound on the merits of silverside, topside, thick flank

. . . like rampant Iceni . . .

and gammon, speak passionately of beef from Scotland and lamb from the West, and even rhapsodise over scrag-end from nowhere in particular. They enjoyed widespread fame. Discerning carnivores from distant Pinner and far away Watford made pilgrimages to Mr Foster's; Ruislip rump lovers came to him; flesh-eaters in Stanmore knew of his name, and Northolt housewives praised him. So too, did the boys from Harrow School; and the vicar of St Mary's blessed him. Mr Foster, he allowed, sold splendid meats, but he regretted the lack of reciprocal business. Mr Foster, he reflected sadly, was never seen in his establishment. However, he did agree that had it not been for Mr Foster I might never have come to Harrow-on-the-Hill and discovered its Mother Church and yes, the Lord *did* move in mysterious ways, didn't He? He was a saintly, sensitive, white-haired man with an aesthetic face and praying hands like those in Dürer's drawing, and like so many Anglican clergymen he 'pride to Gud' and spoke of St Jun; but he was a fine shepherd, and although his flock on the hill were fortunate in having Mr Foster to satisfy their physical cravings, they were double blessed by having the former to attend to their spiritual needs, both in and out of St Mary's. I grew very fond of him and his church, and it became my place of worship for many years.

I could see its spire from my flat in Kenton. Thirty-five minutes walk away, and beyond the green of the playing fields of Northwick Park and Harrow School, and crowning the tree-clad hill that rises from the midst of the borough which bears its name, it has stiletto-ed to the heavens for five hundred years, threatening to pierce the lowering clouds of winter and the mackerel skies of

106

summer. John Lyon, who founded Harrow School lower down the slope when the first Elizabeth was on the throne, would have glanced upward to it on his way to worship in a still ecclesiastically uneasy England. It towered over Sheridan as he went to his classes in the reign of George III; Trollope had it in his sights 150 years ago when, as a day boy at Harrow, and despised as such by scholars and masters alike, he trudged unwillingly toward the school and persecution; and before him, in the same century, a supine adolescent Byron, versifying upon a tomb in Harrow churchyard, watched it flicker through the sighing branches of old elms.

The elms have gone now, victims of the Dutch disease, and aphid-sticky leaves of limes shade the spot where Byron dreamed. Gone too are the views of St Mary's and the school chapel which Kenton folk could once enjoy. Now they are blotted out by a monstrous rectangular glass and ferro-concrete jungle of a hospital, an inferior cubist painting of a building with adjacent shoe-box nurses' quarters. My walk to church would take me through its grounds, out to the traffic noise of the busy double lanes of the Watford Road, across it to the football fields of Harrow School and along a cart track lined with oak and chestnut trees, and then up and up steep Football Lane, climbing between new unmellowed buildings of the school, and so to the top of the hill.

I enjoyed that walk, arduous though it was. And romantic that I am, early one summer morning when the air was fresh and the sky was blue, and dew still glistened in open roses, I saw the scene as it must have been in bad Lord Byron's time. No hospital distressed the skyline and in its place was pastureland, rich with clumps of English

107

oak. As in a dream I heard a stage coach rumble down an unmade Watford Road to London Town, and smelt the dust that its passage left; and in the fields beyond, dotted with yellow ricks, smocked farm workers rested their weary arms on wooden rakes and watched Suffolk Punch draw haywains. It was a pleasing, sylvan fantasy and one I carried with me into the church that fine June day. And the past stayed with me as I sat alone and day-dreamed in a high-backed pew, waiting for the celebrant, and conscious that my watch was fast.

I saw so many ghosts that morning, kneeling and making their orisons below the high timbers of the roof, finely carved from the oaks of Harrow's forests 500 years ago and spanning a nave two centuries older. Past Harrovians, saints and sinners; pious Victorians oblivious of the poor, but socially alert to the need to be seen at public worship; gouty Georgians with fat round bellies and lice-infested powdered wigs, Elizabethans in hose and doublets, all came to make their peace with the Lord. I saw uncompromising Becket – determined not to render to Caesar the things that are God's – kneel in prayer at the altar steps as he did on his way to Martyrdom twelve days before he was butchered by Norman swords and his blood ran red by a chapel pillar in Canterbury; and in my mind's eye, Archbishop Lanfranc glided through the great west door to stand beneath the chancel arch and raise his arms in blessing on the church that he established . . .

Silently, here and there they flitted, those wraiths from bygone centuries, until one by one they melted into the shadows and passed through the flint-faced walls, and I was awakened from my reverie by the tolling of the bell. But it had been a strange experience sitting in the present and surrounded by the distant past, and a poignant reminder of the power and endurance of the Cross of Christ. For despite the schisms, and the wounds and atrocities committed in His Name by Christian bigots, the faith holds fast; and the faithful still muster on Harrow Hill as they did nine hundred years ago.

'My dear Jun,' cried the vicar, beaming behind his rimless glasses and holding my hand warmly between both of his as he greeted me outside the porch at the end of the service, 'Gud's in His heaven today, is he not?' 'Indeed he is,' I said, as a chaffinch sang in a nearby hornbeam, 'and here at least all's right with the world.' 'Yes,' chimed in an elderly lady at my elbow, happily familiar with the quote from Browning but less sure of its authorship, 'Byron wrote such lovely verses, didn't he? But oh!' she continued, looking toward the place where the poet's bastard daughter Allegra Clairmont lies buried, '*what* a debauched man! *So* unmoral! But there we are Vicar, they're all the same aren't they, these artistic people? I mean, I'm told that even in the BBC they . . .'

Her voice faded as I drifted away from them, moved by her mention of his Lordship's name to stroll toward the railed tomb of a gentleman named Peachey. Covered with yellow lichen and splattered by bird droppings it is not, to cite another poet, a thing of beauty and a joy forever, but it has an historic association with Byron and tourists gaze upon it with reverence.

In life, apart from an aptitude for making money enabling him to purchase a last resting place with an exquisite view, and a ridiculously large stone to hold him in place, it would appear that Mr Peachey was an unremarkable fellow. In death, however, he achieved

109

fame beyond his wildest dreams. Byron sat on him. Frequently. For hours. And close to hand a marble tablet says as much. The Peachey Stone, it advises visitors, was Byron's favourite spot.

I could well understand his love for it. Even now, I thought as I turned my back on the late Mr Peachey and leaned upon a Direction Finder set on a low brick wall opposite his remains, the outlook was a fine one despite the ugly urban sprawl of Harrow-in-the-hollow below me. Far away in the heat haze of the south stretched the Home Counties of England, and on the bronze face of the Finder marred only by the slogan 'Mods are best' and a discarded piece of chewing gum, straight lines fanned out to their cities and towns: Salisbury, Winchester, Oxford and Reading; Guildford and Windsor and mean-sounding Slough. But it was to the tired piece of spearmint that I turned my attention.

Stuck between Farnborough and Fleet, and with a spent matchstick rising from its centre like a miniature flag-standard, it all but obliterated the ancient Surrey market town of Farnham. Clearly some south-eastern exile tired of chewing and overcome with nostalgia had fixed it there as a monument to his place of birth, but the sight saddened me. Farnham men, I mused as I removed the blemish seldom, if ever, behaved so commonly. At least, I reflected, not the men of Farnham with whom I used to travel daily on the train seven years before. But they were another breed of Englishmen – the stockbroking commuters from the south . . .

5

Gentlemen and Players

The Home Counties commuter who patronises the Southern Region of British Rail is a very different animal compared with his suburban counterpart who uses the Metropolitan Line and travels to Baker Street. His destination is Waterloo.

Waterloo Station is remarkable not only for the number of nature's unfortunates who, tanned to a deep mahogany and blessed with permanent conjunctivitis by a quotidian intake of methylated spirits, ironically inquire if one has the price of a cup of tea, but for a genteel lady who seemingly lives in the roof. Apparently hoisted there at dawn and released at sundown, her voice echoes from the rafters prissily advising travellers that: 'Ewing tew inclement warther conditions, passengers travelling on the 17.32 tew Alton, should proceed tew Platform Nane.' I am sure that she crooked her little finger over the handle of her British Railways mug and never failed to pass the condiments in the British Rail canteen; and in the days when I was a regular user of the station I often wondered if she took the disease of British Rail officialese home with her and announced to her husband that it was 'inclement in the lounge' and asked him to 'proceed to ignite the fire'. But much more vivid in my scrapbook of Waterloo memories is the scene which was enacted near Platform 13 one Friday afternoon in 1975.

'I say you!' bellowed a pompous balloon of a man with a burgundy voice and a bloodhound face as he advanced majestically across the tarmac toward a ticket collector engrossed in cleaning his nails with a return ticket, 'I want to go to Weybridge!' The man continued with his life's work without looking up. 'Well you go mate,' he said. 'I'm not stoppin' yer.'

The great bulk trembled and the jowls quivered and concertinaed with rage as the snub struck home, and momentarily it seemed that the Stock Exchange would lose a member. But it was a happy moment in my life if not in his, and I still take pleasure from it despite the passing of the years.

As the Elephantine one disclosed, his destination was Weybridge, but he was not untypical of many of the commuters who made their daily journeys between their residences in the more distant stockbroker belt of Hindhead, Churt and Farnham and their offices in the City. Those too I recalled with clarity that Sunday on Harrow Hill when I was taken back in time and rejoined the ranks of the well-heeled who assembled each morning at Farnham Station.

Spruce, pink-faced and manicured, with nails as polished as their vowels and a regulation half inch of white discreetly peeping from breast pockets of dark, well-tailored suits relieved by carefully adjusted club or regimental ties and each with his bowler hat or Homburg, they stood familiarly in groups, chatting and tapping the ferrules of their furled umbrellas upon the platform, secure and confident in their social uniformity. Each had a folded un-read copy of the morning paper tucked neatly under his arm; each carried an impressive attaché case with multiple brass combination locks; and all were to board the 9.01 from Alton, bound for Waterloo.

Known irreverently by the non-commuting denizens of Farnham as the Spivs' Express, its driver was entrusted with the safe and comparatively comfortable transportation of the cream of the City of London. Lesser mortals from the lower echelons of Threadneedle and Throgmorton Streets caught earlier trains. Similarly dressed but less well tailored and also carrying cases with combination locks often containing nothing more confidential than luncheon sandwiches wrapped in tin foil, they travelled under less pleasant conditions, and more slowly. Many of their trains stopped at Aldershot and most carriages bore written testimony of previous halts at the home of the British Army. Texts, authored and in some instances illustrated by bored British soldiery and composed and executed in the train's toilets usually under the pen-names of Kilroy or Wanker, made fascinating if predictable reading. Many had harsh words to say about the town of Aldershot, offering impassioned but impractical advice to its mayor as to what he should do with it, others particularised about a gentleman named Rupert advising readers that not only was he a non-conformist, but a raving one to boot, but most were economical and pungent reflections on the carnal prowess of Aldershot ladies. By contrast, the carriage walls of the 9.01 were innocent of such outré jottings and adornments. And rightly so. The 9.01 was a conservative train; in every sense of the word.

The Nine-0-One was more than a form of transport. It

was a club, an electrified Reform-on-wheels, and acceptance into it was far from easy. Potential members were closely scrutinised, listened to and vetted, and the slightest deviation from convention resulted in a black ball. In my mind's eye I can still see the lonely figure of a Lloyd's underwriter forlornly wandering toward the far reaches of Farnham platform on a bleak January morning, head bowed and trailing his umbrella behind him. He spoke well, had rowed for Shrewsbury and had been heard to say disparaging things about the *Daily Mirror*, but one eventful day he sported socks with clocks in tandem with suede shoes; and that was that. He ended up a broken man, ostracized and forced to rouse his family at an earlier hour and travel on the crowded 8.16.

As often as not the fate of such outcasts was dictated by the more senior members of the club. Easily distinguishable from their junior companions by age and girth and bearing a marked resemblance to Michelin Men, they held court ponderously at appointed places on the platform and pontificated to their favourites who nodded sycophantically or laughed loudly in concert at their President's sallies. 'Quite so!' they said, or 'Ha! Ha! Ha! I must say that was good old boy! Must tell that to the Bloxhams tonight – we're going there for drinks.' They rejoiced in names like Roly, Winco, Groupy and Bonzo, and *bonhomie* oozed from them. But they knew their places and observed protocol both on and off the platform. The Michelin Men took precedence all the way to Waterloo.

Hippopotamically they entrained, removed their hats and placed them with their umbrellas on the racks and sank tight-trousered and unchallenged into favoured

114

window corner seats. Theirs by Divine Right and virtue of long service on the line, for another club member to take possession of it was unthinkable and only once did I witness such a breach of etiquette. It occasioned an ugly scene which lasted until Surbiton where the blackguard left the compartment and was never seen again. However, worse was to follow.

Almost two weeks later to the day, and still brooding upon the indignity of having had to travel with his back to the engine in an unaccustomed position situated directly over a heating pipe, the recognised heir to the seat was admitted to a private nursing home in Haslemere suffering from a severe dose of piles. Well-wishers returning from his bedside reported him as being tolerably comfortable upon his rubber ring but that he had advanced the opinion that his condition could be directly attributed to the action of his usurper, and had added that, although by no means a vindictive man, he wished the scoundrel to perdition. The relayed intelligence was greeted with noises of sympathy from the members of the 9.01 Club on their next journey to the capital and it was agreed unanimously that the transgressor was a rotter.

Fortunately the outrage was without parallel and on all other occasions a fixed routine was observed. As the whistle blew and the wheels rolled, cigarettes were handed round and lit, views were aired on subjects as diverse as the problems presented by teenage au pairs and rising school fees to the perfidy of the trades' union movement, and general chit and chat was exchanged for a maximum of fifteen minutes. Then, led by their president's example, club members opened the pink pages of their *Financial Times*, cursed the print stains from their *Telegraphs* and

. . . standard bearers of England's upper middle classes . . .

buried their faces in them.

From time to time there might be a muffled 'I see poor Conners has handed in his dinner plate' as the President reached the obituary column, or 'The Travers gal popped a boy on Tuesday' as he turned to the birth announcements – desultory bulletins provoking a chorus of 'mms' like those from a glee club tuning up, but in the main, and excluding coughing fits, the only sound to fall upon the smoke-filled air between then and Waterloo was the rustle of turning pages. Once there, as one man they folded their newspapers, replaced their hats and straightened their jackets; as one man they marched purposefully toward the ticket barrier to the canned strains of the Radetsky March from speakers in the roof, and as a unit made their way toward the Drain to bull or bear the hours away until evening assembly on Platform 8 – proud standard bearers of England's upper middle classes, and bastions of the City. And there the ritual would begin again.

The President, dyspeptic and full of business lunch and heavier still with business claret, would close his reddening eyes and snore, open-mouthed and nodding, into oblivion; and his *Country Life* would slide from his lap. His intimates, less favoured with another firm's expense account and thus denied his blessed state, would fight against the hypnotic rhythm of the wheels and watch, from under drooping lids, the passing of the Canada geese on Ash Vale's waters, to be jolted into full consciousness at Aldershot, one stop before their destination. There, gently and dutifully, they would urge their leader from his torpescense, politely inquire if he had had pleasant dreams, discreetly suggest he adjust his dress, and

118

generally assist him to be in full working order by Farnham. Then out they would get with a 'Goodnight' here and a 'Goodnight' there and a 'see-you-tomorrow-D.V.-old-boy', and into their waiting Rovers and Jags and station wagons smelling of dog (Oh! rich Retriever, oily Lab, damp with algae-green Wey water) and so to the steering-wheel-tapping wives, impatient of listening to Radio 4.

'My God!' they would say as they pecked their spouses, 'What a day it's been, what a day that was!' And their wives would smile sympathetically as they switched on ignitions and let out clutches and drove away through leafy lanes to Crondall, Tilford, Frensham, Elstead, Wrecclesham, Rowledge and The Bourne.

They were a contented coterie, and understandably so. Their lot in life was a happy one: Farnham and its environs, as estate agents are quick to point out to prospective settlers, is a highly desirable area in which to root. Particularly if one's political views veer to the right. Here, they will say, you will feel at home.

Remarkable for having produced William Cobbett to whom we are indebted for his *Rural Rides*, and one Augustus Toplady, a Calvinist divine who, bravely bearing his unfortunate surname to the end left us 'Rock of Ages' – a mournful legacy about which many have reservations – Farnham is not an unattractive town, although much has altered since Cobbett put pen to paper.

The incursion of Messrs Sainsbury, Boots, Woolworth's and Smith (W.H.), to say nothing of Curry's, Bejam's and Key Markets, have done little aesthetically for the borough; and traffic has chased the eighteenth century into the side streets. Moreover,

Farnham has expanded unprettily in the south-east, engulfing villages which fifty years ago retained their own identity. But that is progress. However, as Instituted Women sing at the opening of their village meetings, England's land is still green and pleasant in that part of Surrey. Despite the multiplying of mock Tudor bricks which annually eat away its grass and pinewoods, nightingales still sing in Surrey copses, and in surrounding villages ex-naval captains and army brigadiers still insensitively bellow the lessons from Anglican lecterns at evensong and matins. No settlement is without at least a brace of these stalwarts, and some are blessed with many. The village in which I made my home in the early sixties had five. It also boasted an admiral and two generals. All gave valiant service to the community.

On weekdays they busied themselves with the Boy Scout movement and the Special Constabulary; sat on committees and stood at meetings; organised fêtes in aid of the local Conservatives and other more charitable institutions; unfailingly supported the cricket team through thick and thin on Saturdays; and on Sunday afternoons, after pre-luncheon drinks, they donned panama hats and played bowls on the green. They were a great asset, and the appearance of their names and ranks on the electoral roll ensured that the village enjoyed a commanding social position in the rural league, easily beating others in the region who could only muster a cluster of colonels. All are gone now, to command celestial divisions or sail the uncharted seas of space, but when they were alive they were the backbone of the village and much respected by their agrestic fellows in more lowly stations.

Only once did one of them fall from grace. Returning in

the small hours from a naval reunion in London, the Admiral drove his dilapidated Hillman Minx through the by-ways of the village with his eighty-year-old finger on the horn button and a bobbing balloon tied to its bonnet, shouting, 'up the Marines' through his starboard window. Steering erratically past the house of the local GP – a humourless evangelical with a Board school background and a seat on the PCC – and still in fine voice, his progress was seen and logged by that worthy. However, fortunately for the former, the good doctor, retaining a strong sense of feudalism and an awareness of his relative position in the social register of the village, did not disclose his observations publicly but confined himself to whispering them privately into privileged ears over glasses of medium dry sherry. Nevertheless, the disclosures caused ripples on the village pond; and had it not been for the timely activities of a non-conformist vegetable grower who was discovered *in flagrante delecto* among his own brassicas while his wife attended a Bring-and-Buy in the Methodist Hall, the ripples might well have grown into waves. As it was, the Admiral's lapse was totally eclipsed by that of the tradesman, which made much richer copy and, with two exceptions, was enjoyed by all.

The village was seldom bare of drama. In true rustic tradition, everyone knew everything about every other body's business, or quickly fabricated information if they did not; small happenings were inflated to matters of great moment over brass cleaning in the church; harmless gossip was exchanged over pints in the pub and stewed tea in the Women's Institute; and reputations were made or marred by those with idle hands and busy tongues over elevenses and shortbread. But it was a happy, caring

121

community with no more vice than any other in the district, and with more goodness than in many, and when after eighteen years within it I left for London, I did so with sadness. At heart I am not a townsman. Unlike Dr Johnson who once remarked that when a man is tired of London he is tired of life, I am not enamoured of capital cities in which the strain of life is etched in every face and where bird song is drowned by traffic noise. Which is why I still pine for that Surrey oasis.

It was not a beautiful village, and property developers have made it less so than in my day, but it had a certain tranquillity. In it I could hear a blackbird sing its requiem to a dying day and watch a sky become pregnant with stars instead of neon signs; I could walk unhurriedly across a road undisciplined by traffic lights; and in it I could smile at a stranger without having my motives doubted. Above all, I had time to stand and stare as W. H. Davies bade us do.

I once heard Evelyn Waugh say: 'When I was young almost everything was beautiful; now you have to hunt it out like a flea.' He was a tired, unwell man when he made that pronouncement and, I think, an embittered one; but he was wrong. Beauty stares us in the face, and nowhere more so than in the countryside of England. Even in winter. And it was on a winter's morning one December that I saw English beauty at its unique best.

It was a Sunday, and bitterly cold on the Surrey/ Hampshire border. I rose well before the sun had topped the horizon and stood outside my cottage and saw my breath steam into the morning air. Overhead, the last stars clung to a cloudless sky, great Arcturus in the Bear Driver orange and prominent among them, and Venus, white-hot

122

and blazing with the fierceness of phosphorus, shone out in the south east. And as she paled and the light grew stronger, the whole landscape, brittle with frost, sparkled like a sea of diamonds. Old spiders' webs, long vacated by their autumn spinners, were filigreed; every blade of grass became a diamantéd miracle and the delicate tracery of leafless trees was tinged with silver grey.

I turned my greatcoat collar up and walked slowly down the unmade pot-holed lane toward the church, and with every step I took I witnessed the birth of the day. Second by second the sky brightened until it was so full of gold and silver that it seemed that the vaults of heaven must be quite bankrupt; and I stopped in awe of the splendour of it, gazing upward and lost in thought.

'Bootiful ain't it?' crackled a voice behind me, and I turned to the old man who owned it. Close on eighty-seven, and a Norfolk man by birth, he lived near the end of the lane, and despite his years and arthritic limbs each Sunday found him at the altar rail to ''ave a little ole drink with the Lord' as he put it.

'An' some folk say there ain't no God,' he went on. 'Well bugger me,' he said, 'Oi racken they orter stand here with us, don't you my ole boy?' And I nodded in the growing light, and walked with him to church.

He was a fine old man with hands as gnarled as the vines he used to tend in the days when he was a head gardener in one of the big Sussex houses, and even in old age his blue eyes twinkled from his leathery face. He died in his early nineties and I am sure went straight to heaven and to his God with whom he talked in his earthly garden. His faith was very simple and his theology Aristotelian. So far as he was concerned there *was* a 'home for little children above

123

the bright blue sky'; and one for little old men too if they had behaved themselves. But he thought the sputniks had no right up there, 'messin' about with they hangels'. And he said as much to the vicar.

Devout old Jack said many things to many people; and he never minced his words. His general vocabulary may have been impoverished, but his command of basic English was indisputable, although I never once heard him blaspheme. He spoke his mind, and did so that December to a sour-faced woman in the village store who announced that Christmas was a waste of money, and meant nothing to her. 'Then it bloody orter,' he snapped,''cos it's the time when little ole Jesus was born – and don't you bloody forget it. And', he added, glaring after the lady as she departed hurriedly clasping a packet of artificial snow, 'it's my bloody birthday an all.' And he turned to me and chuckled. 'That told her,' he said. 'Stoopid ole besom.'

I know how he felt. I too look forward to Christmas, and to birthdays. Eagerly. My own falls three days before the festival and there was a time when I believed that all the preparations preceding it were being done especially for me. 'How wonderfully kind', I mused when I was six, 'of people to go to all this trouble', and not even the advances of elderly aunts with bristly upper lips which rasped my cheeks as innocent of razor as their own, and their, 'this is for your birthday *and* your Christmas, dear' robbed me of my happiness. Over half a century of Decembers have passed since I entertained that childish notion. Some were spent in Kenya; some in India; and some in Switzerland. But none, not even the ambience of the Bernese Oberland, produced the wonderful magic of Christmasses spent in

124

that English village.

I hold many memories of them. Of the Primary School Nativity Play in the Village Hall when catarrhal shepherds bellowed 'follow the star', and perspiring Magi tripped over their robes and Malchior's make-up ran; of the year Baby Jesus's head came off, and a tearful Mary was clobbered by Joseph; and the never to be forgotten Advent when the inn keeper departed from his script. 'Come in,' he cried to the inquiring couple, 'there's plenty of room inside!' 'Sod me,' said old Jack from the back of the hall. 'That's buggered it up for sure'. And the Head Teacher tore her hair in the wings and the curtain came down on bedlam; and everyone clapped and voted the play the best they ever had seen.

I remember too, the carol singers. For me, there will always be the mystery of sudden voices in the dark, however indifferently they sing. But there they sang well outside my cottage before taking their bobbing storm lantern on a pole down the lane to another house. And the smells of a country Christmas remain with me; the pungent, saturnalian scents of holly, laurel, mistletoe and fir; not stale apologies with withering berries and tired leaves bought from London barrows at inflated prices, but freshly cut and taken from the countryside to decorate the church on Christmas Eve.

Christmas Eve! The one day in the year when the word 'bedtime' did not ring unpleasantly in my children's ears. To climb the stairs on Christmas Eve was no hardship for them, but an embarkation for the land of hope and expectation which the following day would bring with its ecstasy of promise. When the parcels and packages stacked round the tree would be handed out, and even the cat had a present. And the air would rustle excitedly with the sound of tearing paper as the gifts were opened and their secrets revealed: '*Is* it . . .?' 'Can it be . . .?' 'Oh! *just* what I wanted!' And the same wand-clutching fairy that topped the trees of my childhood would stare open-eyed and at a drunken angle at the happiness below her.

Christmas is the child's time, and rightly so. But I remember those Christmas Eves for the walks with my wife to the little church close to the woods, and the ringing of its bell for the midnight mass; for the candlelight and the crowded pews, and the extra chairs which narrowed the aisle for the 'twice-a-yearers' to sit on; for choirboys' faces, pink and shining from over freshly laundered ruffs and with the devil scrubbed out of them for an hour; for the singing of carols which everyone knew, of 'Adeste Fideles' raising the roof, and the joy on the face of the vicar. 'Happy Christmas!' we cried out, one to the other at the service's end, and some of us embraced. Then, out into the night we would go, chattering and laughing, and back to separate homes. But we had worshipped as one family. As old Jack said to me the year before he died: '*That's* Christmas my ole boy – not bloody *Xmas.*'

So winter passed, and the earth warmed. Spring danced in wearing daffodil-yellow and arabis-white, the chaffinch and the chiff chaff called, and the dawn chorus, that forty minutes of liquid exuberance, was heard again. May slipped by, cows drowned in seas of buttercups, and the cuckoo changed his song. But another noise was borne on the breeze; the sound of willow on leather, and occasionally leather on bone. Summer had arrived with its customary wetness, and soon the air was filled with the

126

unforgettable English smells of drying pitches and drying flannels, as village cricketers took the field.

Although a Yorkshireman might be loath to admit it, and even bite the Headingley turf, cricket owes much to Surrey; and to Guildford in particular. For it was in that now architecturally ruined county town to the east of Farnham that the game was first mentioned by name.

'We did', said one John Derrick, gent, when giving evidence in 1598 over the rights of a plot of land, and recalling the days of his youth spent upon it, 'runne and plaie there at crickett and other plaies.' And he was fifty-nine. Moreover, he put it in writing. With two T's.

History does not relate whether John Derrick, gent, was a hard hitting batsman or a devilish bowler. It could be that he was allowed to play merely because he was good at finding the ball in the long grass, but we shall never know. Sixteenth-century score cards are hard to come by in the Guildford area. Nor are they plentiful in Farnham; but in the surrounding villages there is an abundance of data about the local gents and players of the nineteenth century. Of Tilford men like 'Silver Billy' who was born in Wrecclesham and coached by a gingerbread baker from Farnham. And to good effect. As an historian recorded: 'Whenever the ball was bowled at him, there she was hit away and in the most severe, venomous style, and upon my life their speed was as the speed of thought.'

Silver Billy's proper name was Harry Beldham, and when he died in 1862 at the ripe old age of ninety-six, he had played for All England twice and unbroken 'great' cricket, as Lillywhite called it, for thirty-five years. But Tilford men still hit the ball severely, and they are no less venomous in Wrecclesham and Rowledge, or in any of the other village grounds. True, the ball does not always go where the strikers and bowlers intend but the games are fun and played in good spirit; and that is how it should be.

The village cricket match is an English institution, and as permanent as poverty. During the period known laughingly as summer, no weekend will pass without the playing of a fixture somewhere. However, closer to Farnham Town there was a yearly event which was no less noteworthy. It was the annual encounter between the Bat and Ball Inn and the Sandrock Public House, Boundstone; and I treasure the day I first witnessed one.

Wisden has no record of this contest, and few outside the county know of the occasion. They are the poorer for their ignorance. However, an informed minority, the cognoscenti of real rural cricket, spared no effort to attend the spectacle. Nor, as I was to discover, did aficionados of real rural ale. They too supported this unique divertissement and could be seen following the play intently, if glassily, through the bottoms of pint mugs, and evidencing their unwavering and concurrent devotion to both disciplines.

Easily recognisable by the permanence of a glass in each hand from one of which they sipped steadily between deliveries, and only replenishing the empty vessel at the end of each over, their concentration and synchrony was marvellous to behold. But like all zealots they paid a price. Indeed, as still incredulous observers of past events advised me prior to my first-hand enlightenment at the festival, they well remembered seeing many leaving the ground so emotionally disturbed as to be unable to give a coherent account of the day's play, an inability which, my informants added, was also shared by some of the players.

Theirs was a rash assertion, and one which reached the ears of both publicans whose hostelries I visited in search of truth on the day of the match. They were not well pleased. The statement, they said, was a foul calumny, a mendacity. And their knuckles showed white on their beer pumps. In his bar at lunch time, the licensee of the Sandrock was vehement in his rejection of the canard.

'No one from here', said he from the centre of a group of players, 'is allowed more than three pints each before they take the field. Right lads?' he inquired from his surrounding team mates. 'That's right,' chorused the posse of innumerates around him, 'three only!' 'All except him, that is,' continued their captain, nodding toward a stocky individual who was preventing the bar from falling down, 'he's only allowed two. He's got to be careful, he has.' 'Oh,' I asked, 'who's he?' 'Wicket-keeper,' said the captain tersely, 'his eyes go funny after two. Fourteen extras off the first over last year there were. *And* eleven off the second. Weren't there, Patrick?' he called out to the gentleman under discussion. The maligned one paused in his intake of ale and raised two of his fingers in salute. 'Get knotted,' he said pleasantly, and returned to his tankard.

'All the same,' said the captain returning the gesture without rancour and apparently unconcerned by this show of indiscipline, 'we still won. You see,' said he, 'we've got the bowlers. And', he continued, raising his voice above the hub-bub of the fast filling pub and the rapidly emptying glasses as well-wishers poured in to support their heroes, 'we've got enthusiasm on our side, we're abounding with it – we'll stuff them rotten! Won't we lads?' he shouted. 'Yes,' cried everyone in unison, 'we'll definitely stuff them! If they're lucky it'll rain!' And they gave three cheers and said rude things about the Bat and Ball.

I was much impressed, not only by the show of confidence and support, but by the realism of the Sandrock's captain. Whilst clearly aware of his bowling strength, he was not unmindful of the team's Achilles' heel, the wicket-keeper's tendency to double vision. And as I noted the artistry and ease with which that person despatched a pint, I appreciated his anxiety. But the aura within the Sandrock was one of jollity and not concern, the happy Sunday atmosphere of an English country pub, but which that day had a more than usual sense of togetherness. What spirit, I thought as I left them, some flexing their elbows in vertical motions, others with their arms around the waists of lady supporters and, in the case of the wicket-keeper, performing both actions at once – what verve!

I turned into Bat and Ball Lane and walked toward the inn which bears its name. From a nearby church a clock chimed out the quarter. Two-fifteen, and less than an hour to the match. Outside the Bat and Ball a beflannelled young man with a cricket bat drove an imaginary ball toward me. 'Good luck,' I said, entering into the spirit of the mime and returning it to him. 'Do you think you'll win?' He gave a slight twitch and looked uneasy. 'I'm not sure,' he said dubiously, 'not at all sure. I understand the opposition have acquired some very forthright bowling talent.' He licked his lips. 'I'm not very good against pace,' he said; and instinctively massaged his groin. Clearly he was apprehensive – the fact that he executed late cuts all the way to his ear suggested that; and when I went into the Bat and Ball, happy and full as that was too, I sensed just a little edginess at the bar.

Unlike the Sandrock, the Bat and Ball's team was not captained by the publican but by a legal gentleman upon whom greatness suddenly had been thrust. 'Yes,' said that Man of Law, sipping timorously and frequently from his half-pint glass, 'we had a committee to decide who would play, I went away for the weekend, and when I came back I found I was captain! Just like that! Ha! Ha!' He giggled nervously, drained his glass, and showing signs of extreme agitation disappeared into the lavatory to much applause from his fellows, and instructions to have one for them. 'Strewth!' said someone. 'Three bogs in two halves? Bloody hell. Nerves, I suppose.' 'Um,' said another, 'same last year. Remember? Made more runs that way than he did in the middle. And he wasn't even skipper then.' And they laughed uproariously.

Minutes later their leader reappeared, marginally less tense and waving a sheet of toilet paper. 'Batting order,' he cried, 'just worked it out! Have a look at it chaps, and then let's go!' 'Right-oh,' roared the chaps as time was called, 'but do up your flies – it's cold outside!' And to the sounds of 'Land of Hope and Glory' and cries of 'the Bat and Ball for ever!', they departed for the field by divers transport together with their salivating St Bernard mascot.

The chaps were correct in the appreciation of the weather. Outside, the wind was easterly with a bite in it, and as I started off briskly on foot to the Bourne Cricket Club, on whose ground the match was to be contested, I wondered what part the climatic conditions would play in the game. Three pints of beer on a cold day could, I conjectured, cause problems to the fielding side.

Particularly to the Bat and Ball captain; and the Sandrock wicket-keeper. And thus occupied, I continued on my way, curbing my prurience and reflecting that my questions would be answered shortly.

The Bourne Cricket Club has a pleasant oak and fir-lined little ground a ball's throw from the Churt–Hindhead road, and by the time I reached it the teams had arrived; so had their supporters, and so had the beer. A very great deal of it. Promptly inspected by the umpires and other interested parties with the welfare of the game at heart, it was pronounced to have travelled well and to be no worse for its fifteen-minute journey to the ground. That important formality completed, and after only a brief hiatus while the Bat and Ball leader visited the pavilion, the two captains, together with the umpires, inspected the wicket. And so did the St Bernard mascot. The first-mentioned expressed concern about the follow through marks from a previous game, the umpires discussed the specific gravity of the beer, and the St Bernard, showing considerable interest in a leg stump, removed its varnish in five seconds flat before being led off at the gallop to a great ovation, and still smiling.

With the return of decorum, the toss was made, won by the Bat and Ball who elected to field, and the quartet, spearheaded by the Man of Law, jogged from the field exchanging good-natured insults and obscenities as they went, and reported to their dressing rooms. Above them in the roof, scorers sharpened pencils and adjusted their bifocals, the crowd buzzed with expectation, and five minutes later eleven comparatively strong men and true took the field to cheers, counter cheers and boos, and awaited the arrival of the Sandrock's opening batsmen.

'Play!' said the umpire, and the contest was enjoined.

And what applause greeted the first runs, and even greater huzzahs for the first from the bat. Drives to cover, shots to leg, cowshots, mows and sweeps and misses, all were cheered or jeered or groaned at as minute by minute the drama unfolded. An umpire hit in a tender part was transformed into a boy soprano and had to be given a glass of beer, two batsmen collided in mid-wicket and were offered a similar restorative; bails flew and runs came; and at cover point the Man of Law, offering his hands to a descending skier, neglected to close them at the moment of truth. As one man the Sandrock supporters full-throatedly roared their approval of the lapse and asked him to continue the good work. Two balls later he obliged them even more decisively and to even greater approbation.

'Stupid bastard!' screamed the aggrieved and disbelieving bowler in concert with first slip, 'you extremely stupid bastard!' 'Ha! Ha!' said the newly designated love-child self-consciously, and blew into his hands. 'Touch of the old frostbite,' he shouted rubbing them briskly, 'sorry, chaps!' 'Get on with it,' yelled a voice from behind me, 'and pull your finger out!'

Runs came quickly for the Sandrock, but at a price. More wickets fell as the score mounted: and then came the innings for which many had waited with keen anticipation, that of the Sandrock's wicket-keeper – he who had been instructed to restrict his intake to two pints of ale but who, alas, appeared to have lost his ability to count.

With reluctance and difficulty he vacated his seat by one of the barrels and allowed himself to be relieved of his tankard. 'Kew,' he said thickly, 'ver' kind.' Two well-wishers assisted him to the crease, pointed him in the general direction of the bowler, and left him to it. He survived the last ball of the over but then, in a moment of mental abberation, flung himself in the path of a straight drive from his fellow batsman.

'Oh my God,' said his captain in front of me, and buried his face in his hands. 'That's a certain four he's saved for them – I'll do him when he gets back, so help me I will!' 'If he gets back,' said a realist next to him as the wicket-keeper steered an erratic course to cross for a single, blowing kisses to square leg *en route*, 'he can't even see the bowler, never mind the ball – look at him!' We did; and three balls later watched him sit on his stumps.

It was a short, but immensely interesting contribution to the game and one to be unequalled by any other batsman of either side; but there was never really a dull moment in the innings. It was all riveting stuff. Another wicket fell; the Sandrock captain, obviously distressed by his wicket-keeper's cabaret, made only a nodding acquaintance with the block hole, the Bat and Ball's St Bernard, overcome by emotion, committed an enormity in the outfield, another batsman went in and lost a contact lens but stayed, splendid in adversity, and the crowd hummed with excitement and comment. 'Oh, lovely shot!' they cried as he struck two consecutive deliveries for four and hit mid-off's funny-bone with the third; 'take the other one out and you'll do even better! Well done that man, well done!'

It was one of the best one-eyed innings I have ever seen and he returned to a sea of waving tankards and general euphoria, and was immediately given a pint. And so the overs ticked away. The excitement mounted, and so did the score. With one over to go, a flurry of strokes brought the Sandrock's total into the 170s, then to 181; two more runs were added from the first ball of the last over, the next was lofted – and held. The Sandrock's innings closed at 183 for 6 off the allotted thirty overs; and beer was taken at once.

The interval was a hive of activity. Three men, including the family doctor, escorted the Sandrock's wicket-keeper to a bench where, on medical advice, cold water was poured over his head for several minutes; the missing contact lens was discovered at the bottom of a glass and joyously reclaimed by its owner; and the Bat and Ball captain held a conference.

'Well, chaps,' he began brightly, and avoiding the eyes of those who had put him out of wedlock, 'one-eight-four to win, eh? Think we contained them pretty well, what? Yes,' he continued, 'jolly good show! One or two chances went down, ha! ha!, but there we are – even Homer may nod! Still,' he went on, and departing from the classics, 'there's no pace in the pitch and their 'keeper's pissed – should be a doddle really. And don't forget, chaps,' said he, placing his index finger to the side of his nose and closing his off-stump eye, 'there's always Plan B if things go wrong!'

'Plan B,' inquired a startled supporting bystander. 'What's that?' 'Ha! Ha!' said the Man of Law, and pointed to the perimeter of the field. 'Bonfires', he explained, 'we'll get the people in those houses to light 'em, smoke'll drift over the ground and we'll appeal against the light. Ha! Ha! Ha! Good wheeze, what? Anyway chaps,' he concluded, 'pads on, toss up for who's going to wear the box, and remember – the honour of the Bat and Ball's at stake! Hip! Hip?' he inquired of his team. 'Hurrah!' they responded, stirred by the pre-Harfleur-type exhortation and raising their glasses, 'Hurrah! Hurrah!'

The enthusiasm which greeted the entry of the Bat and Ball's openers was no less than that afforded to the Sandrock's, despite the charisma of their wicket-keeper. Remarkably, and aided by medical science, he appeared to have staged a good recovery, and apart from taking the field accoutred with two left pads and a woman's beret, showed little sign of his earlier extravagances. Nevertheless, the first ball, delivered at some pace by a bespectacled bowler with a suspect action, flew over his head bringing four byes, and cheers from the boundary. So did the second. And the third; and when the fourth was snicked through the hands of first slip to increase the total by three, vulgar singing broke out in the Bat and Ball camp only to be silenced by the sight of a leg stump cartwheeling into the air as their star batsman was dismissed for a duck, and returned to the pavilion accompanied by an unkind chorus of quacking.

Worse was to follow. Pausing only in midfield to avail himself of the outgoing player's box, the new arrival took middle and off and was bowled round his legs for two; his successor hit both his wicket and its guardian with the same stroke, and somewhere a faint heart, acting without the captain's sanction, ordered Plan B to be operated and a pall of smoke attended by an acrid smell of burning rubber began to drift across the ground.

As many a test match commentator has observed, cricket is a funny game, and this was no exception. Within minutes the situation changed and see-sawed. Rapidly,

He appeared to have staged a good recovery

and following a severe attack of stomach cramp on the pace bowler as the cold and beer took its toll, the score rose to 63 for 3. At 73 for 3 the order went out to extinguish the bonfires, at 88 for 5 instructions were given for them to be re-ignited; and then came another recovery. From the centre came the sweet sound of a ball being hit from the meat of the bat followed by the equally sweet sound, to Bat and Ball ears, of a pavilion window breaking as the first six of the match was registered. Two balls later the music was repeated to scenes of wild rejoicing.

'Boi God!' said a red-nosed collarless rustic above the tumult, 'that's a nasty smell of broken glass! Puts me in moind of ole Bandy Crowe, that does. 'It the charch bell 'e did, old Bandy Crowe. Tharty yur ago that were. Course 'e's dead now ole Bandy, but that's what 'e done, rung the bloody bell 'e – '

He broke off as more tinkling and cheering signalled the arrival of another massive hit. 'Cor,' he said, 'e ain't 'arf surproisin' they winders. That's three in'it?' 'And the hundred,' said someone. 'They don't know what's hit 'em in the score box!' 'That's roight,' said the ancient, 'that's brought 'em off their arses. Moind,' he continued ''e ain't rung the charch bell yet, not like ole Bandy Crowe done. They sent a chap called 'Airy 'Arry round to get the ball back I remember. Yaas. Vicur said afterwards it were first time 'e'd seen him near the bloody place. Yaas, he were a right old bugger, 'Airy 'Arry was. But ole Bandy Crowe . . .'

And so the spate of runs and reminiscences continued. The unexpurgated and somewhat seamy life stories of Bandy Crowe and Hairy Harry were unfolded, revealing them to be men whose strength was not confined to their

138

arms alone, and the esurient batsman prospered. His was a splendid innings, rich in inventive strokes the like of which will never be illustrated in any cricket manual and one which even drew grudging applause from a visiting Yorkshireman. But, alas for the Bat and Ball, it was not quite good enough. Stumps were drawn, three cheers were given for the winners and losers, the walking wounded and incapables were led away together with a crestfallen St Bernard; and as the ground emptied, the heavens opened.

'Boi God,' said Bandy Crowe's biographer, 'that'll get in through they winders.' 'Aye,' said the visitor from Leeds as the rain lashed his Gammex, 'dead men are 'aving a right old pee. Just like being a t'ome.'

That evening both teams gathered in the victors' pub, and once again the beer flowed as the match was remembered ball by ball, by all except the wicket-keeper. The Sandrock captain, ringing a bell with one hand and holding a tankard in the other, precariously mounted a chair from where he made a speech, and the Man of Law, now untroubled by tension, responded from the floor of the house. Both opined that it had been a great match, and both were cheered to the echo. And when I left in company with the man from Leeds, the exploits of Bandy Crowe and Hairy Harry both on and off the field were still being related from a smoke-filled corner.

'By gow,' volunteered my companion as we walked to where his car was parked and where I had left mine in the morning, 'that wicket-keeper lad. He's not much cop wi t'bat, or behind timbers neither, but blurry 'ell – he can't 'arf sup ale, can't he?' 'Yes,' I agreed, still marvelling at that gentleman's capacity and the size of his storage tanks, 'he certainly can.' 'Mind you,' qualified my new friend, 'there's nowt to ale in t'south. Cat's piss most of it. Not like it is up north. No offence mind,' he continued, 'but he'd not sup Tetley's like that I'll tell yer – by gow he wouldn't!' 'Ah, Tetley's,' I said, nostalgically and appreciatively, 'yes, I agree – it *is* a good beer. So's Theakston's. And Sam Smith's.'

The very mention of the brews brought the man from Leeds to a startled halt under a street lamp. 'You know 'em?' he asked disbelievingly, incredulous that I was aware of the liquid assets which lay north of the Watford Gap, 'you've supped Sam's?' 'Indeed I have', I said, 'many times. I've drunk it in Harewood, and Ilkley and Otley; in Kirby Overblow; and of course at Headingley. You see', I concluded, 'I know that part of Yorkshire quite well.'

The man from Leeds stared at me through the drizzle with a new understanding. 'By gow,' he breathed, searching for his car keys, 'I'll tell yer summat lad – yer not such a daft bugger as yer look. Nice to have met yer.' And so saying he shook hands with me, entered his car, and drove off.

I watched his rear lights disappear, digesting the accolade which he had bestowed upon me. One thing about Yorkshiremen, I mused as I made my way toward my own vehicle, they have a bluntness of speech and a roundness of phrase which is rare in the south; one always knows where one stands with them. But, I reflected, it is not surprising that history has not recorded many of them having held high office in the diplomatic service.

6

Ridings High

I have a deep affection for the largest of England's counties, and for the folk who live within it. Their hearts are as warm as their weather is cold, their humour as dry as their climate is damp, their vowels as broad as their lonely moors, and once it has been accepted, unreservedly, that one's own particular county is inferior to theirs, they will take you to their bosoms. 'It is not your fault', they will infer, 'that you were born outside our boundaries. It was just bad luck; or God's will.' And masking the pity they undoubtedly feel, they open their doors to you.

They are a proud people in Yorkshire. Proud of their genesis, proud of their heritage; and proud of their names. Names like Rams-, Side-, Shuffle- and Long-bottom. These they bear squarely, and even flaunt them. Lesser men would chop off the bottom and call themselves 'Long'; and some do if they move south and into adversity.

I once met a Longbottom whose relatives had been forced to perform this surgery. Lured to London by the prospect of higher wages, a free Datsun and possible professional advancement, they were, so he told me, discomforted by the southern sniggers with which they were greeted whenever an introduction was effected, and

141

after eighteen months they ended the ridicule and consequently moved more easily in the higher echelons of Peckham society. Even so, I was advised, they were not happy in the region, and yearned for their native dales and homeliness. 'And I don't blame 'em,' said my informant who had been staying with them, 'they're a stuck up lot down there!' And as the train in which we were travelling sped northward on a July morning in 1981, he looked with relief through its windows.

He was a small man in his late sixties with a pockmarked, grey, pinched face and a physique at variance with his name.

'That's right,' he said aggressively, catching me in the act of reading his luggage label from the opposite seat shortly after we had left King's Cross, 'Longbottom! And don't bloody laugh!' And pushing his cap to the back of his head, he began rolling himself a cigarette.

Engrossed in its manufacture, and sniffing with concentration, he teased the tobacco sparingly along the paper with thickened fingers, fashioned it into a thin cylinder, offered it to his lips and glared at me. 'Any road,' he said, licking the gummed edge from right to left and nipping the shag from the ends of the tube, 'Longbottom's better than Shitwell.'

Next to me a middle-aged primly dressed bespectacled woman gave a little jump and eyed him surreptitiously and uneasily across the top of her *Christian Science Monitor*.

'Aye,' continued Mr Longbottom, setting fire to his product with a windproof petrol lighter and snapping its lid with a click, 'I were once at school wi' a Shitwell. Albert 'is first name were. Albert Shitwell. Went through 'ell poor little lad did, wi' everyone asking 'im, did 'e? An' believe it or not – and it's Gospel Truth – in't form above were a Crapper! Aye, Shitwell and Crap –.'

'Ai *think*', interrupted the Scientific Christian sharply through pursed lips, and fanning herself with her *Monitor*, 'thet thet is quaite enough! We are not in the culemaines now!' And fearful of a further excursion down the Longbottom memory lane, she gathered her belongings swiftly together and moved down the compartment and away from Mortal Error.

Tripped in his nostalgic stride, Mr Longbottom sourly watched her progress toward the automatic doors. 'By 'eck,' he breathed, as they parted to admit her, 'I bet she pees eau de Cologne an' all.'

His cigarette glowed red as he pulled on it between finger and thumb. 'See what I mean,' he said, interrogatively, 'stuck up. And', he added, 'daft. Daft as a brush. I've never been down't mine in me life. It were mills. In Saltaire.' He inhaled again, and choked as the smoke hit his lungs. 'Aye Saltaire,' he repeated when the coughing stopped, 'two miles from Bradford.' And he drew, as old men are wont to do, on the memories of half a century ago.

'Those were the days', he reminisced, when a Yorkshire teacake was a meal in itself – 'seven inches across and chock-full wi' 'am' – and a week in Blackpool cost fifty bob. When men sang at their work as they sorted the fleeces, or washed out the muck and the fat from the wool, *and* pinched the backsides of the broad-bottomed lasses who finished the fabric or tended the looms. Oh aye! Many a bum he'd tweaked in his time, but he'd never got owt into trouble. He were always respectable like, *and* so were they; they'd not be bedded for a bar of chocolate, not like they are today. And on quiet summer evenings a-courting they'd go, to a mile away from the solid mills, to the southern edge of Ilkley Moor. Aye! What halcyon days they were to be sure! When Hutton made hundreds and the White Rose bloomed, and the pennant of Yorkshire cricket flew proudly; but above all, they were days when folk could walk the streets at night without being battered or thumped. But now . . .

'By 'eck,' he said, extracting a folded newspaper from his jacket pocket and stabbing at a resumé of the rioting of the previous weekend, 'it's all bloody violence, in't it? Look at it! I were reading it on't tube.' He pointed to the column and followed the print with his forefinger.

'Saturday, eleventh July,' he intoned, laboriously reading the words aloud, 'Walthamstow. Winders smashed and police pelted wi' cans as five 'undred Asians went on rampage. Brixton. Running battles between blacks and police. 'Alifax. Three 'undred white youths attacked ambulance station. Constable stabbed in Sheffield. Police stoned in Bradford. That were all on't Saturday,' he said looking up, 'and on't Sunday they started in Leeds – in Chapeltown. But you see what I mean Mister? Nig-nogs, Pakis, Wogs and skin'eads – they're now't but louts, the lot of 'em, black and white – right across t'country. But it's poor bloody police that cop it in't neck.'

He threw the newspaper angrily on to the vacant seat. 'I don't know,' he said, 'they blame it on't unemployment but there were plenty on't dole when I were a lad, and we didn't play silly buggers. No,' he said, 'we'd 'ave 'ad our arses tanned if we 'ad, and that's for sure. *And* we respected t'police.' He paused, and stared moodily

144

through the window and toward the approaching outskirts of Wakefield.

'Going far?' he enquired as he came out of his reverie. 'Leeds,' I said. 'For t'Test?' he asked. I nodded. 'Aye,' he said, aggrievedly, 'and there's summat else – why in't Boycott captain?' And brooding upon yet another miscarriage of justice he fell silent until we reached Leeds and the parting of our ways.

I was indebted to Mr Longbottom. His appreciation of our changing mores may have been blunt and unsophisticated but racially they were unprejudiced and he turned what could have been a tedious journey into an illuminating one. But in truth he was, as a Yorkshire friend of mine would have described him 'a gloomy bugger'. Nevertheless, I shared his disquiet about the breakdown of order. So too did the taxi driver who drove me to Headingley.

'Aye,' he said, as we pulled out of City Square and left the statue of the Black Prince behind us, 'it's quiet enough now but it were quite a do at weekend round Chapeltown. And in Harehills an' all, what with burnings and lootings and such like. Papers reckon there were a million quids' worth of damage done up there.'

I asked him how the trouble started. He shrugged his shoulders and crossed over the Headrow. 'God knows,' he said. 'Some say it were whites coming in from outside, and some say darkies. But any road, between them they made a right mess of things, I'll tell yer. There were a car set alight in't Bayswater Road and a sex shop gutted in Chapeltown. Aye,' he went on, 'police copped four lads pinching mucky mags from it. And in Roundhay Road they're all boarded up – they've not got a winder between 'em. And', he continued, jerking his head toward the Civic Hall as we passed it, 'it's given them an 'eadache an' all, by gum it has.'

Halted by traffic lights, he eyed me in his driving mirror. 'D'ye know it round 'ere then?' he asked. 'Aye,' I said, falling into the local affirmative, 'I've friends in Allerton Park. And in Alwoodly.' 'Oh aye,' he said, affectionately, 'Alyidly! That's what we call it. All big 'ouses and noses up there. And brass. Still', he went on, as the lights turned to green and we drove up Woodhouse Lane, 'it takes all sorts, doesn't it? I've nowt against Jews and I've nowt against blacks. Live and let live, that's my motto. And when all said and done', he continued, 'they're decent folk on the whole, are blacks. And by gow', he added admiringly as we met the Otley Road, 'they can teach us a thing or two wi' t'bat! And so can bloody Aussies – even with our Geoffrey in't side.' And like the lugubrious Longbottom, he too turned broody at the mention of the hallowed name of the patron saint of the Ridings.

'Any 'ow,' he said, as we reached the ground, 'have fun. Chris Old may pick up a wicket or two, but I've not much faith in't rest of bowling.' He cocked his eye skyward in the direction of the Pennines and the gathering grey behind them. 'Aye,' he said, 'wi' a bit of luck we'll be saved by rain – we've not 'ad owt for three weeks.'

My taxi driver, whose name was Arnold, proved to be a good weather prophet. After only one over, fifteen shadowy figures left the field as the clouds lowered and the light dimmed. A quarter of an hour later the rain arrived in torrents.

'Ayoop!' said a red-faced, stocky man next to me,

146

'drought's over! Nowt for it now but to sup ale and wait.' And together with several thousand others we splashed our ways to the bars.

It was a splendid day for the Yorkshire brewers but not, alas, for England. Arnold's prognosis was proved correct. When the sun shone in the afternoon it did so on the Australians alone, and the Yorkshire crowd were not best pleased. They told Botham he was fat and, after he had missed two catches, the name of the nearest optician; they looked disapprovingly upon Michael Brearley from the south, suggesting that not only did he leave their county, but the country; and whilst singing new and vulgar words to the Yorkshire anthem 'On Ilkla Moor ba 'tat', they employed gestures made famous by another Yorkshireman, namely one Mr Harvey Smith. Only Messrs Old, and Boycott (the rightful heir to England's cricket crown), were spared derision. And as the Australian score reached 200 for 3 and the beer can piles on the boundary grew, so Yorkshire voices swelled in harmony and hops, and Yorkshire bodies swayed to and fro, enjoined in brotherhood, brown ale and county chauvinism. And in the Harewood Arms where I stayed that night that sense of pride was echoed.

'I am', pronounced a short fat man with a rumbling catarrhal voice and several stomachs, the lowest of which was controlled by a belt, 'proud, immeasurably proud, to belong to Yorkshire! By gum I am!'

'So', said his friend, who by contrast was thin and immaculately dressed in a double-breasted blazer and who was also engaged in preventing the bar from falling over, 'am I.'

He repeated the declaration and raised his pint in

147

salutation to his county. 'There's nowt like Yorkshire ale, there's nowt like Yorkshire lasses; and by 'eck, there's nowt like Yorkshire countryside!'

'I concur, Derek,' agreed his companion with whom I had passed many a happy hour in the same venue over a number of years and who rejoiced in the name of Oswald Boocock, 'I heartily concur. I've not seen any more beautiful. Anywhere. And', he added in measured tones and addressing me directly, 'we all get very, very annoyed at the attitude taken toward us, by the media.' He paused impressively. 'Don't we Derek?' 'We do Ossie,' said Derek solemnly, 'we mos' certainly do. Very annoyed.'

'You see, my dear Jonathan,' pontificated Oswald Boocock rolling onward, slowly and sombrely, and swaying a little toward me, 'as far as they are concerned, the north is all mills . . . stone houses . . . whippets and, and –'

'Flat 'ats?' suggested Derek, drawing inspiration from another sip of his Tetley's. 'Exactly,' approved Oswald. 'Flat 'ats. And that', he said, 'is all . . . is all –'

'Bollocks?' proposed Derek, ever ready with *le mot juste*. 'Precisely,' said Oswald, 'balls.' ''Ere! 'Ere!' said Derek; and emptied his tumbler.

'You see,' reiterated Mr Boocock, reaching for his own glass and finding it more by luck than judgement, 'people in Yorkshire are just as, as, er –'

'Sophisticated?' prompted Derek. 'Thank you,' said Oswald, 'as anywhere else. Oh yes, oh dear me yes! And another thing too,' he continued, involuntarily taking a step backward before halting and recovering the lost ground more rapidly, 'we have read, and have heard, about the Scots and the Welsh wanting to secede, and run

148

their own countries. And to us, as Yorkshiremen, it's a farce! *They*', he declared, breathing heavily, 'are not *matched* with us! Are they, Derek?'

'No way,' endorsed Derek loyally, albeit thickly, 'no bloody way at all. We've got all the coal we want –'

'And food,' said Oswald.

'And ale, Ossie,' added Derek contributing to the inventory of essentials, 'don't forget t'ale.'

'And', cried Oswald Boocock, producing his trump card, 'we've got Geoffrey Boycott! *We* could secede tomorrow, and *they* would be fighting to get in! But of course, my dear Jonathan,' he concluded, and here his voice dropped reverentially, 'if we did secede, it would only be under Her Most Gracious Majesty, Elizabeth the Second, of England! And if', said he, peering meaningfully into his glass, 'I had summat to sup, I'd drink to Her Glorious Name . . .'

Because at heart I am a masochist, I have the happiest memories of the Harewood Arms. Not to be confused with Harewood House, a larger, unlicensed but better kept establishment just across the Leeds road which runs through the village to prestigious Harrogate with its elderly ladies and Pekinese, who desecrate the crocus beds in spring, it was charmingly mismanaged by a retired Indian Army colonel possessed of a distinguished service record and shiny boots, and an equally polished wife. Now it is the property of a firm of Yorkshire brewers who have, as they say, 'done it up', and I have no first-hand knowledge of the place since modern man moved in. But during the years I stayed beneath its roof, it had an ambience of faded gentility and a reputation not dissimilar to that enjoyed by the fictional Fawlty Towers. At one time it even had a Portuguese waiter.

Named Carlos, he too had charm but, unfortunately for the diners, poor hearing. Consequently one was never quite certain that what one had ordered would actually arrive at the table; and not all were appreciative of the excitement of the unexpected which his malady occasioned. Eventually he left, taking with him the good wishes of kitchen staff and a selection of unmatched serving spoons from the dining room, and returned to his native land. There, overcome by the emotional reunion with his family and an excess of duty free in-flight drinks, he fell down, broke both his legs, and was never heard of again. Meanwhile life went on in the Harewood Arms.

Large and rambling, with a coaching house atmosphere and built of porous grey Yorkshire stone, its exterior walls were covered with Virginia creeper, and omnipresent condensation within. Innocent of central heating, such warmth as there was in the upper regions of the building was supplied by electric fires, the elements of which sparked and hummed with age when switched on and were often accompanied by the smell of burning flex. Antiquated bathrooms were made Turkish in style as the hot air met the cold, mirrors steamed and windows misted; and a nocturnal visit to a distant lavatory forcibly brought home reminders of the rigours faced by Amundsen and Scott, and the courage of those gentlemen.

Such journeys were to be avoided at all costs, but if of necessity they had to be made, the excursions of the discomforted were signalled throughout the house as, below good quality but worn carpeting, old boards groaned, creaked, quivered and sprung, betraying the comings and goings. Little could be done in secrecy in the

Harewood Arms. Not even in the bedrooms. These too had tell-tale floor-boards. And bedsprings.

They were spacious, gracious rooms with ill-fitting Georgian window-frames through which the winter wind whispered to the occupants and, on occasions, howled in anger. Each contained a giant pedestal wash basin, a hunting print or an Arcadian landscape hung on a fraying cord above a tall mantlepiece dressed with Victorian bric-à-brac, two or three chintz loose-covered chairs, and a large, very comfortable bed furnished with soft pillows, crisp cotton sheets, and a satin-covered eiderdown. If nothing else, one always slept well in the Harewood Arms. One was loath to rise in the morning and go downstairs to breakfast. Nor did one have to do so. One could always eat in one's room.

Until her death, room service in the Harewood Arms was provided by an elderly housekeeper who, after a discreet tap on the door, would appear at the foot of the bed together with a teenaged acolyte bearing a laden tray, and a grudge against society.

Peremptorily instructing her serf to set it upon an unstable gate-legged table, she would tiptoe across the room like an overweight ballerina on points, swish open the heavy, faded curtains, wish one good morning, and advise one not to let it get cold. Then, haranguing the misfit for spilling the coffee, she would smack his head and propel him through the bedroom door and away from the quality.

When she died, in harness and a firm believer in the feudal system to the end, her room service duties were taken over by a grey, angular and very ugly Yorkshire lady with a broad, raucous voice, and immensely powerful

. . . *like an overweight ballerina on points* . . .

limbs. Her name was Elsie, and she came from a small town near Bradford called Pudsey where, so I was advised by Mr Boocock, the crows, uncaring of where they are going to, fly backward in order to see where they've been, and where wire-netting is erected to keep out the wind. And he laughed as most Yorkshiremen seem to do, at the very name of Pudsey. 'Aye,' he said, 'Putseh!'

Elsie's room service technique differed greatly from that of her predecessor. Elsie did not tap on the door. She rained blows upon it, shaking it into submission.

'Are we awake then?' she would bellow, as unaided she backed blindly into the room at whirlwind speed and spun round like a top to set the tray down with a crash, 'we'd better be luv – yer breakfast's 'ere!' And bustling across to the windows she would attack the soft furnishings and rip them apart. 'By 'eck,' she would yell as light flooded the room, 'it's brass monkey weather this morning I'll tell yer! Still, it's alright for some, in't it luv?' she would continue rhetorically, as one peered gummy-eyed and disbelievingly at her from over the top of the bedclothes; and giving the eiderdown a friendly wallop, she would speed to the door and slam it behind her. Ten minutes later there would be a groan of hinges and a rush of cold air as it swung open to re-admit her.

'All ri'tarweh luv?' she would enquire, 'ave we done then? No? O-keh luv, don't worry – I'll luke back in a couple of minutes or so. O-keh?' And once again the paper napkins on the tray would rustle as the breeze disturbed them, and the windows rattled and trembled. And as good as her word she would reappear, on time and no less energetically, seize the tray with its half-eaten toast and butter pats, and clatter her way downstairs.

Elsie did not approve of a leisured approach to one's first meal of the day: conversely, the staff in the breakfast room below, did. I once completed a third of *The Times* crossword between disposing of my All Bran and awaiting the arrival of my fried eggs, and solved a further four clues before they were joined by some dispirited rashers of bacon, and a sad sausage. The eventual union was not a happy one and after only one demonstration of the ritual I left the table vowing never to repeat the experience. What happened to the fried tomatoes I shall never know; nor was I enlightened about the fate of the mushrooms.

It was not for the food, or the service, that I returned so many times to the Harewood Arms, but for the company of Yorkshiremen who gave me friendship, warmth, ale and anecdote, and for that of Derek, and Oswald Boocock in particular; for these were the tellers of tales, the yarn spinners of the Yorkshire of the past. Especially O. Boocock.

O. Boocock, like all good story tellers, never let veracity spoil a narrative, but I learned much from him as nightly he stood before the impressive row of beer pumps in the bar, all of which he knew by name. Nor had he distanced himself from the output of distilleries further north, and his nose and girth bore testament to his unswerving devotion to both products. But he was a man of considerable intellect and in his three-score years and one, he had accumulated an enviable knowledge of his county.

He told me tales of the Brontë country to the north and west of Bradford; the land of *Wuthering Heights* and Heathcliffe, eerie and vast with endless mists, moors, and Yorkshire stone and slate, where all the year round it's November. And it was he who directed me to Bradford

154

itself, that basin of a city surrounded by hills dusted with snow in the winter months, where Delius was born and Irving died as the curtain came down on Tennyson's 'Beckett'.

'Into Thy hands O Lord,' he had cried, one October night in 1905; and then gave up the ghost himself. But few in Bradford know of that, and the Theatre Royal in which he spoke those closing lines is now a cinema.

Bradfordians are by no means philistine, but unlike Leeds, Bradford lays no claim to being a cultural centre. It is a city in a pit, a world of money, mills and business where all men, or so it seemed to me, appeared to have been sired by J. B. Priestley. On all sides I saw bulldog faces with heavy eyelids drooping over unsmiling eyes – the sons, grandsons and great-grandsons of the kings of the old wool towns – straight dealing, thrifty self-made men in wrinkled waistcoats with two straining bottom buttons who seemed to be saying to the world in general: 'Life's bloody awful, but we're here to make brass!' And their voices growled from the backs of their throats as they spoke of their city of Bratford.

I would hesitate before playing poker with a Bradford man. No doubt if you prick him he will bleed; if you wrong him, assuredly he will seek revenge; beyond question he is probably as emotional as any man between Land's End and John O'Groats; but he conceals his feelings admirably.

It is very difficult to know what a Bradford man is thinking. Nor does he radiate fun. But, hidden beneath the Bradfordian mask, there lurks a marvellous, dust-dry sense of humour, a wit as distant and flat as the Bradford voice which, to my ear, is so different from that of the

155

West Riding county districts. There the speech sound is warmer, slower and more soft. Moreover, to the uninitiated, many words sound foreign.

In parts like Heptonstall, near Halifax, the elderly still ask 'What dus thee ail?' and not 'What's up?' And some still lace their boo-its and not their boots; and long may they do so. May the dialects of England live on no matter whether they be from the north, the Cotswolds, or the west, for they are music of England, the poetry of our shires and counties. The open vowels of Norfolk; the 'thic' of Dorset; the burr and 'yur' of Somerset and Devon; and the broad sound of the West Riding. All are part of our heritage and we are the richer for them. Inevitably, some sounds will go, and some words will fall into disuse. Our language will continue to evolve as it has since the age of Chaucer, and before; but many will stand the test of time and not be allowed to sleep. Oswald Boocock, for one, will see to that.

'You see, my dear Jonathan,' said that worthy, leaning back on his heels whilst addressing me weightily one Saturday November night in the Harewood Arms and reaffirming his love of Yorkshire, 'as far as I'm concerned, despite the, the machinations of our, bloody, bureaucratic, *clowns*, we still live in *Ridings*; and not, bloody regions!' He looked to his friend for confirmation. 'Don't we Derek?'

'We do, Ossie,' affirmed Derek, nodding in agreement, 'that's where we live. In Ridings!'

'Thrithing,' said Oswald impressively, 'that's the word that Riding comes from, thrithing.' He half turned his head toward me, confidentially. 'Anglo-Saxon you know.'

'And thrithing', said Derek, not wishing to be left out of the tutorial, 'means a third.' 'Precisely,' said Oswald, suppressing a burp, 'that's just what it means. Pardon me. But,' he continued, 'it's a lovely word, is that. Very, very Yorkshire you know. Oh yes.' 'Aye,' said Derek, lowering the level in his glass, 'it is that. Like, mouldywarp for instance. That's another, is mouldywarp.' I looked puzzled.

'Moles,' rumbled Oswald, following the example of his friend, 'and I do not mean the Whitehall variety. Oh no. I refer of course', he continued, 'to the diggery, diggery delvets of this world – those engaging little creatures in black velvet who bugger up our bowling greens, but who are otherwise very lovable. Oh yes,' he repeated, 'very lovable indeed'; and once again addressed himself to his pint. 'But', he said, as he came up for air, 'that's not a word you hear in the south. Is it?' 'No,' I agreed, 'we don't.' 'No,' said Derek, 'you wouldn't. An I'll tell tha summat else' he went on, becoming more Yorkshire by the minute, 'we don't 'ave fleas oop 'ere neither. Do we Ossie?'

'Cer-tainly not,' said Oswald; and drained his glass. 'Lops,' he advised me as he set it down on the bar, 'that's what we've got – lops.' 'Aye,' said Derek, putting his glass alongside Oswald's, 'good, Yorkshire lops!' 'Quite,' said Oswald. 'You see, my friend,' he continued, with mock pomposity and unbridling his third stomach, 'we in Yorkshire retain, and are proud of, the words of our glorious forebears. *They*, will never be, cast upon the scrap 'eap of o-blivion nor be allowed' and he paused, 'to gather dust. Which is more', he added, bringing the oration to a close and eyeing the empties on the bar, 'than can be said

for the present treatment, afforded to our glasses.' And
turning toward me, he raised his eyebrows. 'You take my
point,' he said. 'Oswald,' I said, 'I do.'

That evening, like most I enjoyed in the Harewood
Arms, was a splendid one, and as the hands of the clock
above the fireplace in the bar inched round the dial, so the
company multiplied, the conversation grew and
prospered, and with the passing of the minutes so my
knowledge of Yorkshire lore increased.

From Derek I learned that his old granny had known a
ladybird as a cushy-cow-lady, and had called an idler a
dawkin; from O. Boocock that 'by gum' was derived from
gumption which itself sprang from gaum ('old Gothic you
know lad – it meant understanding'), and from a tall
cadaverous looking gentleman who joined us bearing with
him a half-filled glass of Theakston's, that wakes in
Yorkshire were not what they were.

In appearance he was the epitome of a stage undertaker,
and his voice matched the image. 'By gum,' said that
individual in monotonous tomb-hollow tones, 'it were a
right concern fer't folk in them days were a wake. By gum
it were! They'd bring t'coffin out ut parlour and in tut road –
luvly brass 'andles it 'ad an' all – and put on't bowler 'ats,
and get 'em all mixed oop like. Oh aye,' he went on, 'they
did that.'

He paused, enjoying the memory. 'D'ye know,' he
said, 'Ah once saw a chap wi't wrong bowler 'at on. Ah
did. And by 'eck it were right cutting 'is lugs off! Aye,' he
said, 'it were. And Ah thawt, Eeh! I thawt, if Ah wait long
enough I might coom across t'fellow that's got '*is* on. But
Ah never did. No.'

Regretfully and lugubriously he sipped his beer. 'But

all the same,' he continued reflectively, 'it were all very respectful like tha knows – all luvly an' black an' that. And they'd start off at top of street and wander down, nice and slow like, an everybody'd line oop as they passed their 'ouses and then get in't queue and follow 'em down tut church. An parson would say what a fine lad 'e were and that sun 'ad shone out of his arse; an' after they'd all 'ad a bloody good cry about 'im, they'd get sat down at funeral tea and stuff themselves wi' 'am. Oh aye,' he concluded, ostentatiously and noisily finishing his ale, 'it were a right good do, were a funeral.'

'True' agreed Oswald, studiously ignoring the narrator's empty vessel, 'they may not have thought much about 'em when they were alive, but by God,' he added cynically, 'they didn't half make a fuss of them when they were dead!'

The sepulchral one looked at him mournfully. 'Oh aye,' he said, 'but that's life. In't it?' And with a final glance into his unreplenished glass he set it down upon a nearby table, and drifted away through the smoke.

An hour later the others followed him, the colonel politely reminded the remaining non-resident customers of the licensing hours, invited me to join him for a brandy in his sitting-room, and little by little the bar emptied. Glasses were washed and put away, a guard was placed before the dying embers of the fire; and from the kitchen came the sound of crashing crockery as Elsie dropped her last plates of the day. 'Blurry 'ell,' she yelled as the din died away, 'that's fow-er!' And peace came to the Harewood Arms.

It was close to midnight when I left the colonel. With Remembrance Sunday a few minutes away, he asked me if

159

I would be attending the local memorial service. I shook my head. 'No,' I said. 'I'll be going to church of course – to the 8 o'clock at Kirby Overblow; but I won't be at matins.'

He looked at me, quizzically. 'No,' I said, 'I know it's silly but I always find the reading of the Roll of Honour a little too much for me, wherever it takes place.' He nodded, sympathetically. 'Yes,' he said, 'I know what you mean.' I moved to the door, opened it and turned to face him. 'If it's fine,' I said, 'I'll keep the Silence by myself; in Harewood Park. Goodnight, colonel'.

Upstairs in my bedroom, I pulled aside the heavy drapes and cleaned a circle in the condensation on the window pane. Outside, the Leeds Road, now traffic-less, shone damply in the moonlight, and beyond it I saw the silhouette of trees in the grounds of Harewood House. Somewhere in the distance a dog barked at the waxing moon; closer at hand an owl screeched; and then there was silence. But as I stood there, looking out into the night, in my ear once again I heard the sound of the Hercules and Merlin engines of Halifax and Lancaster bombers as they droned toward the Wash, and the North Sea's black loneliness. And I thought of my friends in Bomber Command who some forty years before had flown under that moon and above the moors to Dresden . . . Berlin . . . Stuttgart . . . and I shivered; and went to bed.

The frost was heavy that night, and when I rose at seven next morning, preparatory to going to church, the countryside was crisp with it. 'By 'eck it's parky!' said a duffle-coated man at the end of the service as he blew into his cupped hands outside the porch, 'but at least it's dry. It'll be a lovely day I reckon.' And together we watched the sky turn pink.

By the time I set out for Harewood Park the whiteness had gone from the land, and I walked under a sun which shone from an ice-blue sky. Down a little lane I went, skirted by a pine plantation on my right and with stone-walled, rising, bush-covered ground on my left, out into the open parkland dotted with sheep and black-patched Friesians standing like toys in sloping green fields, past the outcrop of Ormscliffe Cragg, granite-grey on the distant skyline, and then turned southward toward the climbing sun and to the lake of Harewood House.

It was almost a quarter to eleven when I reached its verges and strolled along them, my hands thrust deep into the pockets of my British Warm, and listened to the subdued quacking of mallards and tufted ducks coming from far across the untroubled waters. The lake is a fine breeding ground for water fowl.

Closer to the bank, a moorhen neck-jerked its way erratically across the surface with a single cry of '*kaak!*'; and from the rushes and reeds ahead of me a coot, disturbed by my approach, sprayed itself hysterically across the water and disappeared below it with a plop. I stopped to see if I could spot its periscope of a beak, but the sunlight dancing on the ever widening ripples made it impossible for me to do so. Instead, I looked around me at the autumn leaves of the chestnuts, beeches and maple trees, and marvelled at the colours as the sun touched them, turning the russets and reds to burnished gold. Not for the first time in my life, I thought how good it was to be alive.

I kept my private silence at eleven, and for two minutes it seemed that the world was still. And as I stood there,

EE-K

alone with my thoughts, three flight of duck came over – a vast assemblage of seven hundred birds or more. In they came, and the wind rush reached me as they passed overhead. And as they hit the lake with a Chop! Chop! Chop!, a huge formation of Canada geese flew in, low and with a steady beat of wings, and in extended line. It was, I thought a great flypast in memory of the fallen. No 'Last Post' or 'Reveille' had been sounded; there had been no recitation of Laurence Binyon's poem. But when eventually I turned my back on Harewood lake and wandered home, I knew that the memory of that Remembrance Day would be slow to die. And I said as much to the colonel. 'My dear fellow,' he said, 'I know exactly what you mean'.

The colonel always said he knew exactly what one meant.

The following day – and with much regret – I said goodbye to my friends in the Harewood Arms; to Oswald and Derek; to the colonel and his lady; even to the undertaker manqué. Indeed, so great was my emotion at parting from them, that in a moment of mental aberration I kissed Elsie. Twice. In the kitchen. But I did not leave Yorkshire. I went to Wharfedale, to Ilkley. I had to. I had a Great Aunt in Ilkley. A very Great Aunt . . .

7

Yur 'tis

My visit to my Great Aunt was a memorable one. A frail, petite, abstemious woman of advanced years, and an enthusiastic hypochondriac to the end of her life, she had, on the day prior to my arrival and on the advice of her general practitioner, stimulated her jaded appetite by taking a little sherry wine. It was a beverage for which she did not much care, but mindful of her doctor's instructions she overcame her antipathy toward it and added a quarter of a bottle of Bristol Cream to her trifle. Twenty-four hours and several spoonfuls later, the effects of the *mélange* were still being remembered by my Great Aunt.

'Oh!' piped she, painfully raising her arthritic hands to the ceiling and looking upward with failing eyes, 'such things I saw! Such things you would never believe! Lights of all colours I saw, dear John – reds and blues and greens and yellows! And the angel Gabriel came into the room and blew his monstrous trumpet! And then in a flash I was above the clouds and hand in hand with Peter Pan, and walking in Never-Never Land! Oh such things, such things!' She lowered her hands and peered uncertainly at me from the depths of her wing chair. 'It was', she concluded in a whisper, 'a fearsome salmagundi.' Even at the age of ninety she had immaculate diction and a rare turn of phrase.

My Great Aunt had lived in Ilkley for over fifty years and had loathed every minute of it. She thought the moor was too large and undeserving of having been immortalised in song; and that the town was too small and unworthy of her. Grudgingly, she allowed that the Brontë sisters had made a considerable contribution to English literature, but marred the accolade by opining that the feat was all the more remarkable considering that the ladies came from Yorkshire. She disapproved of Yorkshire pudding and Yorkshire men, finding both equally hard to digest; avowed that the latter spoke too seldom but that she disliked the sound of their vowels when they did; and she was not enamoured of the northern climate nor the northern way of life. Like Merlin the Wizard with whom, if legend is to be believed, she shared several physical characteristics, my Great Aunt came from the west.

A Welsh woman by birth, and possessed of a brilliant intellect and a caustic tongue capable of verbal laceration in three languages, she had collected Honours degrees as others do match-box labels. And somewhere along her academic road between the universities of Wales, Oxford and the Sorbonne, she had also collected my Great Uncle. 'Not that I *tried*,' she shrilled, 'to be round with you I found him a nuisance. But he pursued me from Heidelburg and wore me down in the Louvre. And that', said she, 'was that.'

Sadly my Great Aunt shook her head. 'He had a fine brain,' she mused, 'but no ambition. None,' she emphasised, 'none at all. Schoolmastering in Ilkley was the pinnacle, his life. Ilkley', cried my Great Aunt on a

164

rising cadence and now inspired by metaphor, 'was his *Parnassus*! But for me,' she concluded dramatically, momentarily transformed by Welsh emotion into a quavering contralto and sounding like the late Sybil Thorndyke in the role of Medea, 'Ilkley has been my intellectual graveyard. I long', said she, going over the top, 'for Charon to row me across the Styx!'

Six months later her wish was granted. The ferryman came and bore her away, to where I know not; and nor did she. Theologically she was unsure, and uncertain of eternity. I once asked her how she viewed the prospect of eternal life. She pursed her lips, tilted her pointed nose to heaven, and deliberated. Eventually she broke silence. 'I think', said she, 'that it depends entirely in which direction one thinks one is certain to be going.' And she smiled an acid smile. But if God has a sense of humour – and I am sure He has – she must have gone upward to tax the angels' patience, and to be reunited with her spouse.

By all accounts, my Great Aunt's assessment of my Great Uncle was accurate in every particular. Letters and other unearthed memorabilia confirmed that he was singularly undemanding of life and did not seek academic glory or any other form of recognition. Only once was greatness thrust upon him. No mean cricketer, history and the annals of the Somerset County Cricket Club record that he was once invited to bat for his county; but he failed to reach double figures and was not asked to Taunton again. By contrast, his brothers, Ebdon P. J. and Ebdon E. W., both brave bucolic sons of Somerset and muscular Christians to boot, respectively played rugby and hockey regularly for the county; and for England. Both men are long since dead but their names are still green within the family. So too is the memory of another departed Westcountry uncle; but for different reasons.

Baptised Piers, but known affectionately as Pipey, he was not of my blood, but an inherited Uncle through marriage. An elderly, stout, pink-faced Devonian with deep blue, permanently surprised eyes, he went through life whistling softly and tunelessly through his teeth when under stress, and with the air of a man who knew vaguely where he was but was not sure why, and who felt that he should be somewhere else but could not remember where. Charitably, certain of his relatives suggested that his demeanour was the result of his having fallen from a horse in Rhodesia in the early part of the century and then landing upon his solar topee. My own private opinions were that his idiosyncrasies were immanent and had been manifest long before he mounted the animal, or, that when young he had been pixie-led on his native Dartmoor and had never recovered. But whatever the causes, it was agreed unanimously that Pipey was, as they would say in Yorkshire, a trifle yonderly.

Wherever he wandered, Pipey left his mark. In the Home Counties he caused consternation by lighting his pipe during a service of holy matrimony in the Parish Church of Guildford as the bride said 'she would'. In nearby Bramley he was long remembered by a minor Canon whose sherry he topped up with soda water; and in London, when accosted by a lady of easy virtue in Curzon Street, he afforded her considerable food for thought by advising her to go away adding, agitatedly, that he was a respectably married woman. Further afield he disturbed the serenity of Bath when he was observed backing hurriedly out of a ladies' lavatory in the Landsdowne

Hotel; in Exeter he was pursued from a similar establishment by a fellow Devonian requesting the return of his overcoat and walking stick, and in Truro he incurred the wrath of a retired colonel of the Duke of Cornwall's Light Infantry when that officer returned to his hotel bedroom to find Pipey lying naked in his bath and vigorously using his loofah. It is related that for a moment the two men stared at one another in silent disbelief. 'What the devil!' roared the Colonel, as the truth sunk in, 'What the hell's goin' on?' 'Ha! Ha!' said Pipey, and started to whistle. Then, clambering from the bath and pausing only to drape himself in the colonel's towels and to bundle his own clothes together, he exited damply leaving a trail of wet patches behind him, and still whistling.

The exploits of Pipey are legion, but he was a lovable character and a staunch Westcountryman. His favourite dog was the Jack Russell – that admirable animal bred by an infamous Blundellian parson for hunting purposes; and when unable to afford whiskey, he drank deeply of Devon cider. He knew 'Uncle Tom Cobleigh' from beginning to end, and could sing 'Widdicombe Goosey Fair' as well. And he spoke of the 'dimsey' and never the twilight; and once a year he read *Lorna Doone* and extolled the virtues of Blackmore.

He was a simple man. In his room there were two watercolour paintings. One showed Dartmoor dressed in September reds and purples with Haytor in the background, the other a thatched, whitewashed cottage in Bideford. Before its lattice windows grew hollyhocks and Russell lupins, Canterbury Bells and stocks, poppies, phlox and aquilegia, and roses climbed around the door.

Appallingly executed by an unknown artist whose lack of talent was matched equally by his or her ignorance of the flowering periods of herbaceous plants, the picture was much loved by Pipey. Dreadful though it was, for him it was a crude, romanticised reminder of the Devon of his youth. So too was a piece of granite which, he told me, came from near Princetown Gaol, and an ornamental glass container filled with rich, red Devon soil. After his death the picture was given to Oxfam and realised seven and ninepence, but the jar of red soil was retained, and I have it still. It stands on a shelf in my study and is to me a tangible reminder of the counties of Devon and Somerset from whence my forebears sprang.

When I was a small boy and walked Westcountry lanes in the days when horses pulled the ploughs, and the sound of the tractor had yet to be heard, I would lie on my back in a Devon field with my hands behind my head, sucking the sweet juice from a stem of grass and watching the clouds roll lazily across the sky. And thus I would dream long afternoons away. Over my head I saw great fleets of ships, their white canvasses billowing as they filled with wind and sailed across the blue seas of heaven. I saw whales and fishes and monstrous shapes, and once, a great pitched battle fought between dragons and mounted horsemen as opposing cloud banks swirled and clashed, and strewed the sky with their fleecy dead. I had many fancies in those boyhood days, but none do I remember better than the notion that if I sat in a ploughed Devon field and gorged myself with milk chocolate, there would come a time when I would merge with the good earth and no one would know I was there at all. 'Oh! The bliss', I reflected, 'of perfect privacy!' The prospect of being violently sick never entered my head.

I spoke of this conceit to a friend of mine who hails from Lincolnshire, where the land is flat and black. 'You see', I explained, 'nothing – except East African murrum – stains the hands and flannels like Devon and Somerset sandstone.'

My friend, who it should be remarked has a somewhat cynical outlook on life, smiled. 'Mind you', said he, busying himself with ridding his pipe of dottle, 'there is another theory. I've heard it advanced', he continued, emptying the plug into an ashtray, 'that the colour of Devon and Somerset soil has nothing to do with sandstone. No,' said he, in answer to my enquiring eyebrows, 'the suggestion is that it has been stained red with the blood of the summer tourists.'

I gave him a long look. '*That*', I said, narrowing my eyes, 'was a most unpleasant innuendo.' He shook his head. 'Not at all,' he said affably, 'it's a fact of life – we all feed off one another. And when all's said and done,' he continued disarmingly, 'we've all got to make a living. Haven't we?' And he beamed, refilled his pipe, and stuck his tongue more firmly in his cheek.

In one respect my friend was correct. The wassailing Westcountryman in winter may sigh at the prospect of the invading hordes destined to run rampant through his counties in the sun-blessed months to come, but he is a realist and hides his emotions well. 'Brass from Birmingham', he will remind himself, 'shines just as bright as Devon gold.' And he will shrug his shoulders and bow to the inevitable.

Tourism does play an important role in the economy of the Westcountry. Moreover, it is a successful and highly organised industry. From the moment the Morning Song rings out in Padstow to welcome in the summer during the opening minutes of May, 'Operation Tourist' begins as in the south, the Midlands and the north, the motorised cavalcades prepare to set out.

Down the motorways they go, bumper to bumper and wheel to wheel, and inhaling the fumes from the car in front. But undaunted they press on – westward, ever westward – to where they know the land is bright. Over the soft green hills of Somerset, along the winding Devon lanes, across the Tamar into Cornwall, and all leaving litter in their wake. And the men and women of the west – hotel and Olde Tea Shoppe owners, Ye Handicrafters and Lace Makers, Ye sellers of quaint Joans the Wads – all await them with open arms, and impatient for the opportunity to make mass sales of genuine brass Cornish piskies manufactured in Hong Kong. Moreover, they wait primed with the knowledge that their clients are conditioned before their arrival. They know that through toffee tins and railway posters, television commercials and radio plays, the illusion that the Westcountry is inhabited by rosy-cheeked girls and straw-sucking yokels all up to their eyes in cider and cream, and slightly slow in the uptake, is still perpetuated and cherished. And there lies their strength. 'Aaarh!' they are expected to say, or 'Yurrh!', and then to look vacant. And they do. They play their parts admirably. Particularly in Somerset. And the customer is pleased. 'How rural!' they say 'just like the Archers!' And off they go, back to Solihull and Walsall taking with them a marmalade jar in the shape of a cottage, and a poker work notice saying 'yur 'tis'. 'Aaarh!' says the Somerset man again, and he smiles a slow, slow smile.

170

Possibly because of his unhurried speech, there is a popular misconception held equally in the north and south of the country and emphasised by third-rate actors who, when depicting Westcountrymen produce an unfortunate sound known as Mummerset, that the Somerset man is dull witted. Nothing could be further from the truth. But he does deliberate before he gives voice to his thoughts. And he does say 'Arh'. 'Arh!' is the Somerset man's cry of agreement, pleasure, surprise or pain and, on occasion, flatulence. It is a multi-purpose monosyllable used by all throughout that brave county from the Mendips to the Brendon Hills, and knows no class barriers. Even churchmen employ it. In 1978 I listened to its sound echoing around the calm of Wells Cathedral as the duty sacristan discovered a bent Belgian franc in the offertory box. Later he expounded at greater length about the duplicity of his fellow men, but I was more impressed by his initial brevity. 'Arh' left a greater mark upon me than all his other words; as it did when two years later I heard it used more vehemently by a stockman in Bridgwater when one of his cows trod upon his foot, and lingered. He too elaborated, and the Bridgwater air turned blue.

It was fate and not design which drew me to Bridgwater. In the failing light of a March afternoon and *en route* for the village of Bicknoller at the foot of the Quantocks where dwelt an elderly second cousin, my car was taken ill. Pops and explosions came from beneath its ageing chassis and I arrived in the town in a series of jerks and sought out the nearest garage.

'Arh!' pronounced an oily man as he withdrew his head from under the bonnet, 'gasket! That's what 'tis – 'ead gasket. Arh.' 'Damn!' I said. 'I'm making for Bicknoller.'

'No yur not,' he said, 'least ways not now, mind. Best stay over. Us'll 'ave a look at 'er in the morning. Least ways,' he qualified, slamming the bonnet shut, 'us'll try to. But 'tis market day tomorrow, see. Yaas. Still', he added philosophically and wiping his hands on some cotton waste, 'you might enjoy that mister.' 'Well' I said resignedly, 'it looks as if I'll have to, doesn't it?' 'That's right,' said the car doctor, and directed me to a small hotel.

'Good evening,' I said breezily as I presented myself at the reception desk. 'I wonder if you can let me have a bed for the night? I'm afraid I've blown a gasket. Ha! Ha!'

The receptionist looked at me, unmoved and unamused. 'Aarh,' he said, and allotted me a room. 'From London are we then?' he enquired as he watched me sign the register. We nodded and said we were. 'Never mind,' he said sympathetically, and handed me my key. I thanked him and asked him if I might use his telephone. 'I want to call Bicknoller,' I explained. 'Bicknoller?' he repeated, surprised that I knew of its existence. 'That's wur poor old Harold Gimlett wur born.' 'Yes,' I said. 'I know. And so was my cousin. She used to push him around in his pram.'

His eyebrows shot up and he looked at me with a new-found respect. 'Rear-lay?' he exclaimed, his pupils dancing as he attempted to work out my genealogy. 'Then you'm part Somerset then?' 'That's right,' I agreed. 'In fact my grandfather came from Wellington.' 'Well I never,' said my host elect, now convinced that I would bring no harm to his establishment. 'Well! Well! Well! Well that's all right then, in ert? Yur,' he said, pushing the instrument toward me, 'have it on the house.' And

172

folding his arms comfortably upon the counter, he settled in to monitor my conversation.

'Percoolier things, gaskets,' he said, when I had appraised my cousin of the situation and replaced the receiver. 'Very percoolier. Yaas. Still', he continued, determined that I should look on the bright side and echoing the thoughts of the garage mechanic, 'least ways you'll be yur for market day. Yaas. You'll like that I reckon. Anyhow,' he concluded, stubbing out his cigarette and preparing to show me to my room, 'welcome to Bridgwater.'

As I was to discover, Bridgwater's name is more attractive than the place. Once, so I was told that evening by a friendly, middle-aged red-faced farmer from the Vale of Taunton who I met in the bar, it was tranquil and wealthy, its riches founded on a thriving coal trade. But that, said he, was in Bridgwater's palmy days, a century and more ago. That was when its little ships sailed up the Parrot on which it stands, bringing in salted fish from Ireland and wines from France, and then tied up in the busy Town Reach. But now, Bridgwater was a prosperous industrial town and, he allowed, a pretty noisy one some nights.

'Anyhow,' he said as he finished his gin and tonic, 'reckon you'll see for yourself later – if you'm a mind to go out that is.' He stood up from his bar stool and patted the yellow felt waistcoat under his brown tweed jacket. 'Grub time, I reckon,' he declared, and hitched up his straining twill trousers. 'Care to join us then?'

He was a large, hairy man built like a Suffolk Punch and with bushy red side whiskers joined beneath a bulbous nose by a handle-bar moustache. Seen from the front he

173

put me much in mind of Beatrix Potter's Tom Kitten, and as I followed him into the dining room, marvelling at the width of his buttocks, I wondered if he too, like fat Thomas, would eat too much and burst his buttons; but he was an amiable character, amusing company and, as I had anticipated, a remarkable trencherman.

I learned much from him during the course of our meal and particularly with regard to the morrow's cattle auction. His brother, he told me, would be bringing some stock to it early next morning. 'For killing,' he explained, 'leastways if the price is right, that is. If it isn't us'll take 'em back and try again next week, see?' I asked him what they were selling. 'Lamb,' he said. And tucking his napkin into his collar attacked an ample slice of that animal upon the plate before him. 'There is', he endorsed as he opened his mouth wide to receive the substantial offering, 'nothing like a nice bit of lamb. English lamb, that is,' he qualified with his mouth full, and gesticulating at me with his fork. 'Not New Zealand mind. That's rubbish that is. They do say', he went on through an intake of carrot, 'that they send their best ewes over, but I'm not so sure mind.' 'But it is cheaper, isn't it?' I asked. 'Maybe 'tis,' he said, spearing a potato and admitting it whole, 'but t'isn't English, is it?'

He was refreshingly chauvinistic, proud of his country and of the local farming community. 'Yes,' he said, as he continued the onslaught on his victuals, 'I reckon you won't find a better class of farmer anywhere else in the south-west than roun' yur – nor a better sample of fat stock neither! And', he added, 'buyers know that too – that's why they come, see? Oh yes. Tomorrow they'll be yur from Andover, Kent, the Midlands – all over. And', he

174

'. . . nothing like a nice bit of lamb'

emphasised, demolishing the last morsel and washing it down with some beer, 'they'll have the best auctioneers in the country too.'

He beamed at me across his empty plate, drew his napkin from left to right under his hair forest, and drank again. 'And', he said, repeating the mopping operation and indicating his tankard, 'likely us'll be doing a bit of this, too. Oh yes. At the New Inn,' he specified, 'extended licence on Wednesdays see? Right up to four-thirty. But only for market traders mind – t'other buggers are kicked out at half two!' And he laughed loudly, and picked up the menu. 'Arh,' he said, 'what's next I wonder?'

Two minutes later a portion of jam roly poly joined the English lamb below his waistcoat, and as I waved away the offer of some fresh cream trifle and asked for coffee, I watched him make rapid inroads on a prodigious piece of Double Gloucester. 'Good English cheese,' he pronounced, as he destroyed the last of it. 'You can't beat it. Not when it's fresh like. Not like that sweaty muck you buy in the supermarkets. Oh no. Still,' he concluded reflectively, 'that's a perk of living in the country, in'ert? That an' fresh air. And you don't get that in the towns, that's for sure.'

He sighed contentedly, pushed his plate away and glanced at his wristwatch. 'Half eight,' he announced. 'Time for one more in the bar and then bed I reckon. Busy day tomorrow, see?' I asked him what time the auction would begin. ''Bout ten thirty,' he said, 'for lambs that is. Then old John Titman – he's the head auctioneer like, he'll start the cattle at about twelve, and then 'tis all over by one. But my brother'll be yur by eight or so with our lot, so

Yur 'tis

I best go down and see 'em coming off.'

He scrumpled his napkin onto a side plate, lit a small cigar and rose from the table. 'Mind you,' he said, 'that might interest you – if you can wake up early enough that is!' And chuckling deep down in his throat he put a large, heavy hand on my shoulder. 'Care for a swift 'arf then?' I thanked him but shook my head. 'No,' I said, 'I think I'll stretch my legs for a bit.' 'Ah well,' he said, 'see you tomorrow maybe. Mind how you go then.' And so saying he moved ponderously in the direction of the bar, leaving me to cogitate on the powers of his digestive system, and resolved to be early abroad.

'Enjoy your dinner then?' asked my friend at reception as I handed in my key and fastened the belt of my raincoat. 'Very much,' I said, 'and the company.' 'Oh arh,' he said, 'old Jeremy.' And he laughed. ''E's quite a character 'e is. An' by God 'e can't 'arf eat, that one. Put a bloody ox away 'e can – 'orns an' all. An' in no time. Mind you,' he went on, anxious that I should know of his esteem for my erstwhile companion, ''e knows how to farm, old Jerry does. Oh yes. And 'e knows the district.' 'Yes,' I agreed, 'I learned a lot from him about Bridgwater.' And I nodded to him, and went through the doors to the street outside.

It was not a pleasant night. A light drizzle had set in and the lights of Bridgwater reflected wetly off its roads. I pulled at my mackintosh collar and reminded myself that one does not get the best impression of any venue under such conditions, but the further I walked the less I found to commend the town. To be sure, it had a splendid shopping centre with neon-lit windows ironically displaying advertisements for New Zealand lamb and

EE-L

177

processed cheese – the very articles so despised by the surrounding farming communities – but chainstores have never pleased me. Nor did I enjoy the sight and sound of the crowds of leather-jacketed teenagers who roared up and down the streets on motorcycles, and thence in and out of the pubs. Neither did the Somerset Constabulary. They too were there in force, each faction eyeing the other with mutual dislike and suspicion. Somehow the presence of both parties was alien to the fair name of Bridgwater and I did not linger amongst them.

'Goodnight,' I said as I collected my key and asked for an early call; and morosely climbed upstairs to bed. What, I wondered, before sleep claimed me, would the morning bring? And I closed my eyes and dreamed of broken gaskets and black-faced rams riding Yamahas, and of other dreadful things. But I need not have fretted. The following day I saw the other face of Bridgwater.

The English climate is noted for its fickleness. The west had been cold and damp for two months of the year, but on that Wednesday the sun rose in a cloudless sky and at 8 o'clock the morning smelt of spring. Gulls flying in from Bridgwater Bay cried to each other as they wheeled above me as I made my way through quiet streets toward the market place, and higher still in the cold thin air an aircraft noiselessly blazed a long trail of white against the unbroken blue. In contrast with the previous night, the town was at peace. So, too, was the cattle market. Save for some ubiquitous house sparrows cheeping and hopping beneath the network of metal railings which divided the cattle pens from those of the sheep, the place was empty when I reached it and only my footsteps echoed on the concrete square. Of the hirsute Jeremy there was no sign and I wondered if the Double Gloucester had had its revenge. I reflected also that I could have enjoyed a longer breakfast.

I filled and lit my pipe, sauntering as I did so and taking stock of my surroundings. Above the entrance to the market an iron plaque advised me that it had been declared open in 1935 by His Worship the Mayor attended by several dignitaries whose names were also immortalised below his. Various advertisements proclaimed that there was a Cooper Dip for Every Need, including one for maggot-fly; a very gentle breeze ruffled a peeling poster on a board belatedly reminding me that there had been a Parliamentary Election for Bridgwater in 1979; and as I gazed at it contemplating on who had won the seat, an overweight red setter ambled into the square, lay down and went to sleep. 'Cheep! cheep!' said the sparrows unconcernedly; and I began to conjecture as to whether I had come to the right place.

My doubts were ill-founded. As I stood there with my hands in my pockets and drawing on my pipe, the peace of the morning was shattered.

'Allo boy!' roared Jeremy from a hundred yards distant, his face even redder than the night before, 'made it then, did we?' And simultaneously a cattle transporter pulled into the square. The first candidates for the auction had arrived. 'All right are we then?' bellowed Jeremy. 'Arh,' yelled the driver and his mate, and down clanged the tail ramps on squealing hinges, and down them clattered the cattle. Out they stepped, the first of many, uncertainly and head to tail, some with their heads thrown back and their brown eyes rolling in agitation, but all with breath steaming through wide-stretched nostrils. Seconds later they were joined by others and soon the air was full of the sounds of lowing and blowing and shouting and clouting, and the sweet smell of freshly dropped dung.

'Hey! Hey! Hey!' cried the brown-coated stockmen in green rubber boots as they urged the more truculent from the trucks. 'Ho! Ho! Ho!' shouted others in white coats and trilbies, and slapped numbered labels on the sweating flanks.

Minute by minute more transport arrived, and steadily the clamour grew as sellers met potential buyers. 'Lovely day!' they called to each other. 'First of spring I shouldn't wonder. 'Tis good to feel the sun!' And they waved their sticks and their shepherd's crooks, and clapped one another's backs.

Everyone knew everyone else. 'Busy day I 'ad yesterday, Alf,' bawled a bow-legged ancient to a thin young man in dungarees. 'Two line of peas and a set of onions, and three or four row of spring cabbage. That's what I put in boy!' 'Arh!' his grandson bellowed back, 'an I got in they collys you give I – an' 'ad the Tom seen to an' all.' ' 'Bout bloody time too,' the old one yelled, 'randy ole bugger 'e wur!' And still the lorries rolled in, their trade names written upon their sides, and the meetings and greetings and bleatings continued as the sun shone down on us all. F. Trot appeared on the scene. So did Grabham & Roll. And I thought how aptly entitled they were, and that fact is stranger than fiction. An open trailer off-loaded some sheep, their fleeces pink from Somerset's red soil. Protestingly they were driven into their allotted pens and then, as they were combed by caring hands to make them pretty, with acute insensitivity a High Class Butchers van

180

drew up, and I was glad they could not read.

'Look good, don't they?' I said conversationally through the hub-bub to an overalled shepherd and his friend as together we leaned over a pen full of lambs. Both were short, tubby men with grey stubble sprouting from weather-beaten faces, and their eyes were like those of their charges.

'Arh,' said the nearer of the duo, mesmerised by the sea of wool before him and addressing me indirectly in a soft, slow voice. 'Not bad considering the rain we've 'ad. They don't do do in the wet. They don't put on weight nor nothing see. Not in the wet they don't. Do they Pete?' he enquired of his friend. 'That's right,' confirmed Pete, equally slowly and similarly hypnotised, 'when it's wet they don't do do. Not', he explained, 'like they do do in the sun. That's when they lie around and do do like. Don't they 'Arry?' 'Arh,' said 'Arry, summing up, 'they do do well in the sun.' And stimulated by the repeated reference to the day star he removed his hat, wiped his brow with the back of his hand, and glanced upward. 'Lovely day,' he said. 'Glorious,' I agreed. 'Arh,' said Pete. And slowly scratched his head.

'From London?' asked 'Arry, replacing his trilby. I nodded and said that I was. 'Arh,' said Pete, and sucked his teeth. 'Us went there once.' He paused. 'Didn't us 'Arry?' 'Arh,' said 'Arry, 'just once like. Drove us mad. Ole Pete said to I – I tell 'e 'Arry, if us don't get out of yur he said, I'll die dead. Didn't you Pete?' 'I did,' affirmed Peter, ''an certain sure I would 'ave. Bloody 'orrible it wur.'

For a moment both men fell silent, digesting the horrid memory. Then: 'No offence meant mind,' said Pete.

181

'None taken,' I assured him, and changed the subject. 'Think they'll fetch a good price?' I asked, gesturing toward the woolly innocents. 'Arry gazed at the sheep with ovine eyes, and thoughtfully chewed a matchstick. 'Hard to say really,' he said through the softening wood. 'Last week they were making forty to fifty pounds a piece like.' 'Arh,' said Pete, 'and 260 pence a kilo for spring lamb mind. But us won't know 'til they start selling, see.' 'That's right,' agreed 'Arry, 'that's when we'll know.'

They did not have long to wait. Within minutes of taking leave of them, a hand bell pealed out above the multisonous din, and for sheep and seller and buyer and butcher, the moment of truth arrived. The sale was due to begin.

That cattle market was the first I had ever witnessed, but excluding a tobacco auction which I attended in Rhodesia, for sheer speed of selling I have yet to see, or hear, a better example of that expertise.

'Diddle-um, diddle-um, diddle-um dum dum, diddle-um, diddle-um, diddle-um dum dum!' cried the auctioneer, sounding like a vocalised version of the overture to William Tell as he strung the bids together, 'dum, diddle-up dum DUM!' And down came the hammer on the winning bid, and the next lot came up for auction with scarcely a pause between. It was a remarkable feat of breath control and labial agility and one, I suspect, which could not be performed with dentures.

One by one the sheep were sold. Sucked lambs born the previous December; year-old hogs and sheep lambed twelve months past; all were ear-punctured and ticketed, and led away bleeding and uncaring. Half an hour later, and with no less urgency, came the turn of the cattle. And by 1 o'clock all was over. Accounts were settled; the crowd thinned. Sheep and cattle, oblivious of their fate, were driven away by their new owners to meet their Maker, and gradually the square emptied as in ones and twos farmers and dealers drifted toward the red-brick New Market Hotel by the entrance to the market place. Motivated by the herd instinct and a dry throat, I followed in their wake.

It was when I neared the door of the hotel that I saw Jeremy again. ''Allo there boy,' he boomed, removing a cheroot from below the red fungus and waving an ash stick in my direction. 'Enjoy it then, did we?' 'Enormously,' I said as I reached him and noting how his colouring matched the brickwork. 'Never seen anything like it.' 'Arh,' he roared, seemingly oblivious that the distance between us had closed. 'I told 'e didn't I? Best auctioneers in the West we 'ave! And I'll tell 'e something else,' he said, lowering his voice to a bellow and sweating profusely in the blazing sun, 'they're not the only ones yur today – there's Old Mother Ashe down at the Corn Exchange, proper character she is. Yes,' he continued, mopping his face with a bandanna handkerchief and then blowing his nose stentoriously, 'you ought to look in on 'er before you leave boy – 'tis only five minutes walk away. Then you can come back yur, see? Yes,' he said, stuffing the handkerchief back in his pocket and making for the door, 'you do that – you'll get quite a surprise I reckon!' And with a great guffaw and another wave, he disappeared inside.

Red Bull, as I had dubbed him privately, was correct on both counts. I did reach the Exchange within a few minutes, and Old Mother Ashe did surprise me. Indeed, Old Mother Ashe astonished me. Topped by a dark cloche hat with blue-grey permed hair coming out on both sides and wearing a long thick grey coat which reached down to brown brogues, she was a short little lady with a scrubbed complexion and had, I adjudged, been around for some sixty years. But it was not her appearance which commanded my attention. It was what she said: for Old Mother Ashe had clung on to the past, and auctioned in Lsd.

'Ten shillings may I, for this bedroom chair?' she was asking the motley crowd gathered around her stall as I joined them in the covered market place. 'Do I hear ten anyone?' she repeated sedately, but to no avail. 'Well, five may I?' she urged.

'Arh,' said a man wearing a porkpie hat and a hearing aid. 'Thank you,' said Old Mother Ashe graciously. 'Seven-and-six anywhere? Ten do I hear? Twelve-and-six may I,' she continued against an increasing buzz of conversation in the background and looking encouragingly at the man in the porkpie hat. 'Twelve-and-six?' 'That's right,' he said in a quavering voice, 'ten shillings.' 'No dear, no,' said Old Mother Ashe, 'you'm a bit confused dear. Not that I'm surprised,' she added severely, 'what with all that noise at the back.'

She glared towards the offenders. 'I've asked them to be quiet, but I might as well be talking to myself. I don't know', she inquired of the rest of us, 'how *they'd* like to come here and stand for twelve hours at a time.' Several of us said that we didn't know either, but that certainly we should not wish to. 'That's right,' agreed Old Mother Ashe slightly mollified by the show of allied support. 'You wouldn't. Now where were we?' Collectively we told her.

'Ah yes,' she said, refocusing on the bemused one, 'I think your bid was twelve-and-six, wasn't it?' 'All right,'

184

said Pork Pie, and adjusted his aid. 'Good,' said Old
Mother Ashe. 'Fifteen shillings may I?' 'Arh,' said Pork
Pie, nodding happily, 'arh.'

Old Mother Ashe stopped, sighed deeply, and went
closer to him. 'Dear,' she said sweetly into his earpiece,
'you'm bidding against yourself you know.' 'Poor old
sod,' said a man next to me, 'let 'im 'ave it Missus.' Old
Mother Ashe sighed again. 'Best I do,' she said
resignedly, and knocked the article down.

Fifteen minutes later I bought a knobbly walking stick
for half a guinea.

'I take it you'll accept these?' I asked as I paid up and
handed her a fifty and a five pence piece. She looked at
the coins with distaste. 'Oh yes,' she confirmed, 'we have
to. But I don't hold with them I don't – not one bit. No,'
she continued, 'I think we were done when we had
this decimal.' 'Really,' I said, 'how?' Old Mother
Ashe looked at me pityingly. 'Because', she explained,
slowly and as if addressing a singularly backward child,
'the *old* pound was worth 240 pence, and *this* one's only a
hundred . . .'

When I left she was pinging the bell of a dilapidated
typewriter and assuring her audience that it had worked
perfectly well earlier, and may she have twenty-two-and-
sixpence for it; but it was her numerology which had
intrigued me. Like the die-hards of Sherbourne, who
rioted when the Gregorian calendar robbed them of eleven
days, she wanted her numbers back and would not be
comforted. And thus occupied in thought and twirling my
stick as I went, I retraced my steps along the High Street
and back to the New Market Hall.

The very bones of England were in the crowded inn that

afternoon. Excluding myself, all present were market traders and talk was of livestock, land and other farmers and how well the auction had gone. Good beasts had realised good prices and that, as I was reminded proudly more than once, was as it should be – Somerset offered the best. Young, middle-aged and elderly, all were certain of that; and as time passed and beer gave way to whiskey, so they spiced the air with laughter, ribaldry and the speech of Somerset, burr-rich and thick as cream.

It was all marvellously bucolic, alcoholic and convivial, but paramountly it was essentially English. Jeremy, his features now florid and resembling the centrepiece of a Guy Fawkes' night celebration, put a glass in my hand and piloted me from farmer to farmer, introducing me as he did so as that 'poor bugger from London'. I met the barmaid who, buxom and blonde, answered to the name of Perky and, to her acute embarrassment, was told why. I made the acquaintance of a toothless gaffer who allowed that although market days were not the social occasions that they used to be, only death would prevent him from attending them – a statement which provoked applause from his cronies and a call for him to provide another round before he did kick the bucket – and I encountered an elderly, minute dairyman with a prodigious thirst who bemoaned the falling off in the production and drinking of real cider.

'That's right,' agreed Jeremy, towering over him and taking in a mouthful of shandy, 'they don't use Bramleys now see – not like they did mind with 'ome brewed scrumpy. Arh,' he emphasised, 'now that wur a drink – weren't it Gilbert?'

'Arh,' said Gilbert, lowering his glass, 'an' I mind

when everyone drank it to. T'was a common drink see,' he explained to me. 'Oh, yes. All the farm 'ands like, they'd come knocking for their quart 'for they went out. Oh yes,' he went on, 'din' matter whom yu wur. Ef you'm come banging at the farm'ouse door yu'd get a pint of scrumpy given. *An*',' he continued, emptying his glass, 'you'd be asked if yu'd like another.' 'That's all right boy,' roared Jeremy, all but felling him with a friendly pat, 'no need choke yourself – us takes the 'int!' And requisitioning our empty tankards, he shouldered his way toward Perky.

Shortly afterwards I took my leave of them with many handshakes and regrets, and blessing the gasket which I had so soundly cursed the day before. How strange, I mused as I left their warmth and went into that of the sun, that the failure of such a small component should be responsible for so much pleasure. And I said as much to the garage mechanic, and to the hotel receptionist. 'Arh,' said the latter, looking pleased. 'P'raps you might come back then?' I nodded. 'Who knows?' I said, 'perhaps I might. At least on a Market Day.'

I had no cause to hurry that afternoon, and I motored gently and pensively toward the Quantocks' feet. The day, I reflected, had been kind to me. The sun had shone, and I had been made to feel at home; and perhaps that had been so. Perhaps the ghosts of Ebdons past had whispered into my subconscious ear that the west was where I belonged. Not in London streets, or on Surrey Downs, nor yet in the Yorkshire Dales, but here . . . where the soil is red, and the hills are green, and the gulls fly in from the sea.

Acknowledgements

The author would like to thank the following for their co-operation and help in the preparation of this book: Madame Tussauds Ltd; the London Planetarium; the BBC; Dunhill's; Astleys; Christopher & Co; Berry Bros & Rudd; and *Punch* magazine.